Teacher Agency

This book provides educators with a conceptual framework to explore and develop authenticity and agency for equity. In response to growing cynicism within the field of education, Raquel Ríos argues that in order to become authentic agents of change, teachers must take a stance of mindful inquiry and examine the role of a teacher within the broader socio-political context. By utilizing the six principles of Conscientious Engagement, teachers can expand their awareness of the power of language and thought, the complex nature of our professional relationships, and how we channel energy in ways that can impede or strengthen our work for equity. Full of real-world stories and input from practitioners in the field, this book helps teachers of all levels develop the skills and confidence to grapple with tough philosophical and ethical questions related to social justice and equity, such as:

♦ What is poverty consciousness and what responsibility do we owe students who come from poorer communities?
♦ How does racist ideology impact our thinking and practice in education?
♦ How can we tap into an evolutionary consciousness and collective purpose in order to transform how we advocate for equity?
♦ How can we expand our professional network for the integration of new ideas?
♦ How can teachers really make a difference that matters, a difference that extends *beyond* the four walls of the classroom?

Raquel Ríos, Ph.D., has over fifteen years' experience as a teacher and professional development specialist supporting teachers, instructional coaches, and leaders. Currently, she is an instructional designer at New Teacher Center, a national resource on mentoring and coaching for teacher effectiveness located in Santa Cruz, California.

Other Eye On Education Books
Available from Routledge
(www.routledge.com/eyeoneducation)

Let's Get Real:
Exploring Race, Class, and Gender Identities in the Classroom
Martha Caldwell and Oman Frame

The Classes They Remember:
Using Role Plays to Bring Social Studies and English to Life
David Sherrin

Judging for Themselves:
Using Mock Trials to Bring Social Studies and English to Life
David Sherrin

History Class Revisited:
Tools and Projects to Engage Middle School Students in
Social Studies
Jody Passanisi

7 Ways to Transform the Lives of Wounded Students
Joe Hendershott

Mentoring Is a Verb
Strategies for Improving College and Career Readiness
Russ Olwell

Educating Students in Poverty:
Effective Practices for Leadership and Teaching
Mark Lineburg and Rex Gearheart

Teacher Agency for Equity

A Framework for Conscientious Engagement

Raquel Ríos

Routledge
Taylor & Francis Group

NEW YORK AND LONDON

KH

First published 2018
by Routledge
711 Third Avenue, New York, NY 10017

and by Routledge
2 Park Square, Milton Park, Abingdon, Oxon, OX14 4RN

Routledge is an imprint of the Taylor & Francis Group, an informa business

Library of Congress Cataloging-in-Publication Data
A catalog record has been requested.

ISBN: 978-1-138-30261-7 (hbk)
ISBN: 978-1-138-30262-4 (pbk)
ISBN: 978-1-315-17864-6 (ebk)

Typeset in Palatino LT Std
by diacriTech, Chennai

1/10/18

For

Miguel Vélez-Rossi
My husband and dream keeper

This being human is a guesthouse.

Every morning a new arrival…

Rumi

"People are indeed perfectly uninteresting if they possess no personal powers which can make a difference. Of course, if this is the case, then it is hard to see how they can offer any resistance, for even if it is ineffectual it has to stem from someone who at least amounts to the proportions of an irritant (and must thus be credited minimally with the personal power to challenge)."

Margaret Archer, Being Human:
The Problem of Agency, 2000

Contents

Meet the Author

Dr. Raquel Ríos is currently an Instructional Designer at New Teacher Center. She has extensive experience designing and delivering curriculum and instruction to teachers, instructional coaches and school leaders. She has worked nationally across the United States and internationally in Spain, the United Arab Emirates and Puerto Rico. She specializes in language acquisition, critical literacy, social justice and change leadership.

Preface

This work is an introduction to a new theory and practice designed to help educators examine and develop teacher agency for equity. It is based on my scholarship, observations and concrete situations that span the course of a career as an in-service teacher educator and professional development specialist, nationally and internationally. It includes critical moments in my life that have informed my understanding of agency, equity and the evolution of human consciousness. Over the last decade or so, I have found that teachers are becoming increasingly skeptical about this notion of teacher as change agent for equity. While teachers largely believe they are making a difference in the lives of children and families, many of whom work in high-poverty, high-minority school settings, they are beginning to question whether the difference they are making is really the type of difference that matters. This book is in response to this cynicism, a growing cognitive dissonance between what teachers know to be their authentic purpose as educators and how they are being positioned in schools and society.

An Uncertain Time

We are living at a time when there are overwhelming racial, economic and ideological tensions in our country and across the world. Demonstrations of mass discontent with the status quo and establishment politics have revealed that the current system is not responsive to citizens. People need to be reassured that we are indeed working together for the promise of a democratic society in which all are treated equally. Schools are the microcosms of society and they are increasingly segregated by race and class. Teachers often do not come from the communities in which they teach. Inequality is widening and there is an overwhelming tension around the expectations of market-driven curriculum and instruction policies. All of this characterizes a time that Diane Ravitch coins as "the life and death of public education." The recent fervor surrounding the presidential campaign and election is emblematic of a corporate-controlled mass media platform that broadcasts politicians and pundits who barrage the public with a narrative of intolerance and extreme nationalism, the idolization of the wealthy, disdain for the poor, and fear and contempt for Blacks, Latinos, Native Americans, immigrants, Muslims and women. All of this has teachers across the country besieged with concern. How are we to help our children make sense of this troubling situation? How can we move forward working and supporting schools and communities that are confused and suffering?

Teachers have long been alert to the mounting challenges we face as a society: the cooption of modes of communication, public turned private systems and a new demagogic, identity politics that have over time helped to dehumanize our work as public servants. Now is the time when we as a nation must coalesce around a collective vision and get serious about what we need to do to make sure public education becomes the platform through which citizens can preserve our democracy and learn the knowledge and skills needed to examine the context in which we live in and build a more egalitarian, humane society.

How Can We Move Ahead?

In the wake of a surprising Trump presidency, there is only one way to look at the pathway ahead of us. We need a big change that requires a shift in our collective consciousness, one that can energize a multi-party, multi-generational, multi-ethnic, multi-racial social movement, one that challenges all racialized, class-based and gender-based ideologies. The collective spirit consciousness that I will talk about in this book is an emergent energy that has a great force of will and a readiness that I have already witnessed amongst teachers and teacher educators. Teachers are deeply concerned about the character of our country and recognize public education as a promise that we have not lost our moral clarity.

For a long time, teachers, teacher educators and school leaders have been feeling frustrated that in many cases the sound voice of social justice does not matter and that teachers do not have the power to impact the type of decisions that matter in society. It is true that there has been reluctance within institutions to formally and decisively address the challenges we face, challenges that are often rooted in our own processes that with examination may perpetuate the vast inequalities we wish to ameliorate. We have noticed that instead of changing the questions that drive our conversations, we create more terminologies that have only resulted in distancing ourselves from the pulse of humanity, the dehumanization of our work and a lagging sense of social responsibility. Many of us have been left numb in our sensibilities. That is why, now more than ever we must demonstrate our resilience and communicate a sense of urgency about the realization of our equity goals through this process we call education. It is incumbent upon all of us to find the renewed energy and courage to join the thousands of citizens across the country who have refused to let go of what matters and to advocate for truth, authenticity and equity.

There are many pathways that we can take to arrive at our collective vision for equity, although upon reflection, all pathways share the same foundational elements. I have been humbled by the appearance of literature that speaks to a mission for equity and spirit consciousness amongst educators in particular. This book is one pathway. Its purpose is to help teachers and teacher educators engage in the critical examination of self, the examination of our socio-political context and the examination of the role of the teacher with in it—keeping equity and spirit consciousness at the focus of the conversation. I hope that as you explore this pathway you will find that the ideas resonate with you and so many other voices that are opening up the field. In this work, I am joining the many others who are every day planting the seeds of a new narrative that challenges this notion that poverty and racism are individual and cultural manifestations and instead see poverty and racism as byproducts of our collective consciousness that manifest themselves in public policy, decision-making and everyday practice. As such, we can liberate ourselves from toxic streams of consciousness in order to clear the space for a new energy that can be channeled into new, innovative directions.

More than 15 years ago, Palmer Parker wrote a book called *The Courage to Teach*. In it he argues that in order for us to find the courage to bring our authentic selves to work as educators, we must activate three essential pathways: the intellectual, emotional and spiritual. Several years later bell hooks released *Teaching Community*, in which she writes, "Schooling that does not honor the needs of the spirit simply intensifies that sense of being lost, of being unable to connect." I believe that now is the time to explore our collective spirit consciousness in education—now when teachers are skeptical, cynical or numb. These feelings of uncertainty and frustration point to the fact that we have somehow lost our way or have given up our power as human agents of change. Reclaiming the essence of who we are, embracing our innate wisdom and pouring ourselves into the important work of educating children for a future consciousness is so important.

What to Expect in This Book

In reading this book, you will learn what the examination and development of agency looks like and feels like through my own voice, the voices of educators who I have invited to participate and voices that I have encountered through my extensive research. You will find that much of the work takes the form of examining tough, philosophical questions that put our spirit consciousness and equity at the center of our thinking. Questions like: What is poverty consciousness and how might racist or hegemonic ideologies reveal itself in everyday practice? How does my language and approach to teaching reflect who I think is ultimately responsible for poverty or the challenges we currently face in our society? How might have teachers been socialized to accept mythical images of teachers as rescuers, missionaries and heroes creating barriers to Authentic Presence and reciprocal transformation? What are the hidden dynamics of our working relationships that may impede or strengthen our commitment and work for equity? How can our understanding of the evolution of future consciousness as a source of energy transform how we advocate for equitable learning environments and healthy sustainable societies?

The Conscientious Engagement Framework

Conscientious Engagement is a theoretical and practical framework composed of six interlocking principles designed to help teachers and teacher educators examine and develop teacher agency for equity. They are Spirit Consciousness and Authentic Presence, Entanglement and Freedom, and Meliorism and Emergence. This is a powerful tool. Each interlocking principle helps us challenge assumptions, beliefs and national narratives that prevent us from experiencing our own self-empowerment and realizing our collective vision for equity. It helps make critical connections between everyday teaching and learning and the holistic nature of human development that is grounded in the evolution of our consciousness. This connects interesting fields of study like metaphysics, neuroscience and teaching in a way that can expand our understanding of the mind–body–spirit relationship. On a more practical level, the Conscientious Engagement framework can serve to ground professional conversations, adult learning and development and direct coaching and mentoring professionals. Our work in schools with in-service teachers, Pre-K through 12th grade—as well as our work developing teacher education programs—must include discussions on spirit consciousness and advancements in technology and social science in order to ensure we are current and informed and able to fully integrate new knowledge into the design of learning experiences. This, as you will see, is at the heart of agency—making a difference that matters that extends beyond the classroom and school building. This framework will also help educators nourish authentic relationships across race and class, so that together we have the courage to stand up for what we believe in. It will encourage us to listen to our private, inner thoughts with compassion so that we can free ourselves from limited thinking and release the energy that will move us along a more conscientiously engaged path.

In this book, I examine three big ideas and their implications for practice that I argue are essential for teacher agency for equity. The first is the notion of Spirit Consciousness—an evolution of consciousness that is the energy source that nourishes our vision and efforts for equity. I will discuss how we are collectively moving away from the "I" and embracing the "We," moving towards interdependence and collective purpose. In the field of education, this means moving away from a positivistic stance and embracing an integrative, holistic way of thinking. This shift in consciousness, you will learn, is an energy source that enables us to focus on the big picture and relate our work to our fundamental purpose as human beings. The second big idea is Entanglement. It is about how human beings are largely driven by our primal need for belonging and how our strict adherence to consensus building can often limit our work for equity. I will argue that in order to exercise agency for equity in education, we need to transcend these entangled relationships, move out of our comfort zone and engage with human beings who have a shared life purpose that honors our collective humanity. The third big idea is this notion of Emergence which refers to how we need to conserve and direct human energy in ways that will enable the full integration of new ideas, ignite our imagination and lead towards more equitable practices.

Theory Meets Practice

This book is divided into two parts. Part I, titled "Why Conscientious Engagement?", is the rationale and justification for a new theory and practice for teacher agency for equity. Chapters 1–5, starting with the Introduction, are designed as a collection of essays or commentaries. This approach provides the reader with a broader, more organic presentation of my perspective, which includes insights and observations from my work in the field. In the chapter on Perspective, I provide you with my educational stance as a Mindful Scholar Practitioner and share details from my life that have strengthened my interest and passion for equity in education. Chapters 3 and 4 address two important topics related to equity: Poverty and Racism.

I introduce the term Poverty Consciousness and in doing so reveal the complex relationship between race and class and how it plays out in education. Chapter 5 is the introduction to Conscientious Engagement. In this chapter I weave in real voices from the field in order to support my rationale and purpose for a new approach for equity. I outline the key assumptions embedded in this work and introduce the conceptual framework and the Six Principles for Teacher Agency for Equity.

Part II is a deep dive into the Six Principles for Teacher Agency for Equity. I describe in depth the six interlocking theories and practices that I posit are needed as we examine and develop teacher agency for equity. They are Spirit Consciousness and Authentic Presence, Entanglement and Freedom, and Meliorism and Emergence.

Implications for the Reader

In addition to inspiring teachers and teacher educators to expand their awareness of the inner dynamics of self and of our world with a focus on equity, I also want readers to come away with implications for everyday practice. Each chapter ends with Reflection Questions related to the big ideas brought up in the chapter that will help you make critical connections between theory and your everyday life as a teacher and/or teacher educator. I attempt to frame the reflection questions around what I argue are the three ways we operationalize agency. They are through (1) thoughts and language, (2) relationships and (3) how we channel our energy. The questions are meant to be personal yet broad enough so that regardless of your role or where you are in your social-spiritual journey towards agency, you can use them to ground self-examination as well as discussions with colleagues.

***

As I write this book, the media coverage is concentrated on post-Trump election news that has people all over the world apprehensive. With many radical policies and appointments to key government positions, many wonder if people are ready to respond in protest and what that will mean for our country. Perhaps it is worthy to remember that we have all been witness to darkness, hate, ineptitude and apathy, certainly to different degrees, but still, I wonder just how much of this divisive rhetoric truly reflects our collective consciousness. While it is hard not to feel afraid, I am reminded of the power of a great teacher, who speaks, writes and breathes light into even the darkest room.

It has taken me a long time to come to terms with my own sense of agency. What is it that I can offer the world, when I have so little in terms of money or social currency? I do have intolerance for human suffering and a tireless belief in the goodness of humanity. Both of these dispositions empower me to wake up each day and continue to be engaged—through my writing, my teaching and channeling my energy in ways that allow me to integrate new knowledge and imagine us living a future egalitarian society. This is faith. This book has been the result of many inner and outer journeys and a life-long inquiry into the nature of teaching and learning. It has been a struggle to come to voice and to find a way to give voice to the voiceless. Some days I feel exhausted and I ask, when will this work end? Yet I know this is a quest for love and an inquiry into truth which continues to evolve every single day. So, even today while people have taken to the streets chanting #NotMyPresident and #UnAmerican, I ask myself: What is my purpose? What is the most important thing? How can I honor the totality of our experience and still communicate a sense of urgency for a better future? I find great solace in knowing that more often than not, humankind finds greatness in those moments when we are pushed out of our limit; that in chaos, uncertainty and frustration, we meet up with moral clarity. I hope that as we evolve, we also embrace the possibility that evolution does not have to come from destruction and suffering but it can also sprout out of love. Now I spend most of my days typing words to a page and although I often miss the dynamic, rich life of a teacher, I know I am living out my purpose and I hope that you too will do the same.

Acknowledgements

There are countless people who have been a source of inspiration and support, many of them teachers and students. Without them this book would have never flourished.

I wish to thank and acknowledge several colleagues at the New Teacher Center for their immediate trust, authenticity and willingness to engage. They are Clarissa Williams, Dianne McNamara and Dr. Irene Liefshitz. A special thank you to Dr. Rewa Chisholm, Leslie Baldacci, and Lybroan James for their ongoing reassurance and support during the last stages of this project and to Ellen Moir, Jenny Morgan, Lisa Mount and Ellen Greig for welcoming me into the safe space of our design team.

I would like to express my appreciation to Dr. Heeja Kim, Dr. Xae Alicia Reyes, Dr. Pedro Noguera and Dr. Shiv Talwar for providing me with the academic and spiritual guidance needed— each in their own unique way. I would also like to thank Prof. Richard Gurspan for his wisdom, passion and camaraderie.

I have deep gratitude for my family and friends who surround me with love, support and an intellectually stimulating safe space even when I am lost in my research or writing—especially my husband Miguel, my son Marco and my daughter Natalia, who continue to shower me daily with their divine wisdom and unconditional love. I would like to thank my mother Lourdes Maldonado for her belief in me, her commitment to social work and for passing on an intellectual life; my father Henry Ríos for his steadfastness, sense of humor and lively debate and my in-laws Elvira and Miguel Vélez-Rossi who are my home away from home. I am also profoundly grateful for Voza Rivers, Christopher Ríos, Nerissa-Marisol Rivers and Adrienne R. Palacios for their unyielding faith and attention to my artist soul.

I would like to acknowledge the folks at Routledge, starting with Catherine Bernard who was the first to open the door. I would like to thank my editor, Lauren Davis, who with her gentle partnership, responsiveness and talent has succeeded in bringing this work to a broad audience.

Last, I would like to express reverence to the great mystical force I call God, which is always at the center of all things even as we swirl around and around in search of truth and the miraculous.

1

Why Conscientious Engagement?

1

Introduction: Reclaiming Your Purpose in Education

If you are deeply dissatisfied with what is going on in education, how decisions are made, how things are organized, how media and business interests have skewed our understanding of the purpose of education and muddled our sense of self, especially as teachers—then this book is for you. Deep dissatisfaction with the current reality of schooling, one that breeds fear, hate, powerlessness and despair (all of which I know intimately) can have a profound impact on our physical, emotional, social and spiritual well-being as teachers and as human beings—all of which cripples our capacity to think freely and engage conscientiously in society.

Within every new theory in education there is a prediction. If you have the courage to challenge yourself and the world around you for a better future, you will find in these pages a theory and practice that will help you reclaim your purpose in education and reimagine teaching as a vocation that can lead us to a more humane, egalitarian future. Within these pages, you will find enduring questions that I hope will take hold of you with a passion. They have accompanied me over a lifetime as a teacher and as a teacher educator without respite. The more I learn and know, the more I realize that we do not have the answers to these enduring questions but directing our energy to them should be our primary task; for grappling with the right questions can take us one step closer to understanding this human dilemma we find ourselves in.

The Evolution of Teaching for Equity

One of the primary purposes for writing this book is to share some simple truths about teaching and learning for equity. For some readers, I imagine, there might be difficulty accepting the simplicity of the truths presented here, because simplicity implies that we must do something about it. Often I have worried that our level of consciousness is that of a spectator and we are stuck, paralyzed. I have watched many brilliant minds in education discuss and debate the issue of equity as if the notion of equity were debatable or some exotic artifact needing a new frame. The fact of the matter is that the very nature of equity, like truth itself, only exists in action. It is not static. The words equity and truth are filled with motion, and only in movement do these two things exist. According to Freire, to speak a true word is to transform the world and within the true word, there are always two dimensions, reflection and action.[1] The debate that exists today about education for equity, or the lack thereof, is simply that of static, false words: they are devoid of action and therefore we are left only with an illusion.

Over the course of my career as a teacher and teacher educator, I have observed teachers and those who support them becoming increasingly anxious about the emptiness of equity initiatives in education and their ability as teachers to effect any real change. As a consequence of Trump's shocking election to president, our fears and anxiety about diversity in America and our failure to approach equity initiatives in any meaningful way are now taking center stage. I don't like to talk about silver linings in the midst of real danger, but this recent political debacle has the potential to draw the type of attention to critical issues in our society that is desperately needed. If you are reading this book, you are part of an emerging consciousness that has grown out of this uncertainty, a cognitive dissonance between what we believe as educators to be our true purpose and the reality of how we are being positioned in schools and society. This heightening of awareness and anxiety is palpable—in faculty rooms, in classrooms, in meeting centers and at national conferences. There is apprehension, yes, but there is also willingness and a desire to engage in an honest conversation—to critically examine the role of a teacher in an increasingly inequitable school system and ask ourselves if in some way we have been implicated in the very problems we wish to ameliorate.

Perhaps you are socially, emotionally and spiritually exhausted and so there is nothing left but to consider a new pathway. The evolutionary teacher must activate the mind, body and spirit in everything they do. They also need to situate themselves and their practice within the broader, socio-political context in order to have an impact that matters. This is what it means to be an authentic teacher for equity. If you are not willing to critically examine yourself and the conditions of the world we live in, you will never be a great teacher. When I say a great teacher, I mean someone who can nurture and guide others to reach their true potential, who can perform alchemy with knowledge, who can transmit the deep joy of self-love, inner peace and agency and who can offer compassion and healing for our imperfect humanity.

> The evolutionary teacher must activate the mind, body and spirit in everything they do. They also need to situate themselves and their practice within the broader, socio-political context in order to have an impact that matters. This is what it means to be an authentic teacher for equity.

Teaching and learning is an act of truth and authenticity in relationships is required for it to work. It is ritualistic and ceremonial at times but it is also organic and improvised. It is a skill and also an art. It is a science and an act of faith. To achieve this state of being and doing with equity in mind, we must activate our whole selves—our mind, our body and our Spirit Consciousness. This includes a commitment to Mindful Inquiry as a way to get deep understanding of our collective consciousness, which includes examining the language we use that may limit or expand our practice for equity, the nature of our personal and professional relationships and how we channel our energy in ways that are sure to impact the lives of teachers, children and families. This is the practice I call Conscientious Engagement. It is the only sustainable future I foresee for education.

Where Education Reform Falls Short

Over the last two decades, I have found that we are wrongly obsessed with how to reform teaching and learning with a narrow focus on fixing some people in society. Often in education circles, the question arises: Who are we talking about exactly? The answer is inevitably poor children, children of color, American Indians, blacks, Native Hawaiians, Latinos, Asians, at-risk youth, English Language Learners, immigrants, urban youth, and so on. I have often wondered how even in our free and democratic American society that privileges whiteness, there are still a significant number of whites who are poor and disenfranchised. Are we referring to these children as well when we discuss how we have to change our approach to teaching and learning?

Social-emotional learning or SEL and learner variability have become faddish these days. They have trumped all conversations about equity at the high level. When we talk about Social Emotional Learning, we are talking about the personal regulation of emotions in order to improve how we engage and work with others in society. When we talk about Learner Variability, we are talking about how each child is unique with distinct learning dispositions. Both of these topics are important as we consider how to differentiate and balance our teaching and learning, but neither directly addresses equity and racism. Equity refers to the distribution of resources, competing interests and the abuse of power and racism is the belief that some human beings are inferior. Neither of these important issues is addressed sufficiently, if at all in some cases, in social-emotional learning and learner variability.

For example, I wonder when we talk about social-emotional learning and learner variability, are we thinking about how we should address the needs of the group of white children who grow up armed with hate, believe in guns and will at a very early age come to rationalize the killing of black and brown people to defend their race? When we consider social-emotional learning and learner variability, are we talking about the needs of children who are born into privilege, who attend a good school and are educated in the dominant culture, who are being groomed to emulate parents who often sit in comfortable leadership positions and design policies that perpetuate inequity and institutionalize racism? I am also wondering about the children of academics and pundits who certainly contribute to our knowledge base but who never really seem to touch the ground, engage with the common folks, or take a stand on issues that matter the most to the majority of children and families.

As a conscientious educator who has spent many years supporting public school teachers and administrators, I think a lot about the impact of poverty and the growing economic insecurity on our behavior. According to the National Center for Children in Poverty, 15 million children or 21% of all children live in poverty. This number is based on an income that many argue is half of what families really need to cover basic expenses. As of 2013, nearly twenty million people lived in a state of destitution, which is an increase of about eight million since 2000.[2] Not surprisingly, poverty rates are highest among black, Latino and American Indian children, which is why discussions about equity also require an examination of racist ideology. As a parent and teacher, I am deeply concerned about poor children and families who characterize many of our communities but I am also worried about the mindset of our teachers and school leaders who, like all of us, have absorbed the fear of economic insecurity and who may have adopted attitudes towards the poor that Tim Wise describes as increasingly vicious, hostile or contemptuous. In his recent book, *Under the Affluence,* Wise asserts that because economic inequities are in some ways more deeply entrenched than ever, we need to challenge the false assumption made by many that vast inequalities are natural and inevitable rather than that they exist because of decisions we have made within political and civil society, decisions that can be just as readily undone through collective action once we recognize the source of the trouble.[3] Adam Haslett, who wrote a provocative article in *The Nation* released in October 2016, also makes reference to this phenomenon, but he takes on a slightly different angle. He writes, "we are living a time of gaping inequality and an ever-more-freelance labor market making *economic insecurity—* absolute or relative—a general condition for the vast majority of the population." Haslettt goes on to explain that this economic insecurity is one of the main reasons why Trump has gotten so much attention. It is because he is surfacing a "pervasive feeling of shame that has always accompanied poverty, or not being able to provide all you want for your children, or enjoying less than you see others enjoying, or—in this second Gilded Age—simply not being rich."[4]

Understanding Poverty Consciousness

Raising poverty consciousness is at the heart of working towards and for equity. It is about challenging this pervasive attitude that stigmatizes poor people as misfit objects unenlightened about the ways of the world, a population that is lazy and/or who devalues the promise of education and who is part of a "culture of poverty" that is dependent and accustomed to taking, rather than giving. Our American tradition enforces the notion that individuals have the power to change their own fates if only they put their minds and hard work to it. This is the pulling oneself up by one's own bootstraps ideology. American media hosts like Rush Limbaugh asks listeners, as if the answer were self-evidently negative, if they "know any low income people who actually *want* to get a better job?" and wonders, "Do they even *want* to work?"[5] As a consequence of my own humble beginnings (my grandparents benefitted from public assistance) and policies that helped me access education opportunities, plus like so many Americans, I lost property and income in the economic collapse of 2008, I have spent a lot of time wondering about the character of the poor as compared to the character of the rich. Sadly, in doing this, something tells me that even in this wondering I am doing something terribly wrong, like I too have succumbed to the invasiveness of a predatory-like public narrative. Yet, I wonder and question. I need to examine these things because if I truly believe the purpose of education is about academics and character, then I want to know what kind of character we are building in our country.

As educators, we tell ourselves that if you are born poor, like my grandmother, who had absolutely nothing (may she rest in peace), then you must require a distinct set of educational ingredients in order to grow into a healthy, mindful, intelligent, responsible human being. Strangely, we don't spend much time thinking about how we can make healthy food, water, a home, a safe and beautiful community, appropriate clothing and health care accessible to all human beings. Instead, we deliberate over the best evidenced-based approach to teaching poor children who, by our scientific observations continuously demonstrate failure in spite of our great efforts and therefore should be perceived as 'intellectually deficient' and treated as a social liability.

Well-intentioned educators sit perplexed and frustrated by their inability to solve this thorny problem of poor children who just won't achieve in school. It's as if we refuse to consider the possibility that the answers are indeed so simple and continue to probe the wrong questions over and over again thinking that poor folks are the misfits; rather our questions are misfit questions, and really what we do is pass our time entertaining questions in service to our insatiable academic, egotistical minds. Meanwhile, the world around us seems to be crumbling.

We talk a lot about literacy and mathematics in education. I have visited schools where all other subject books are relegated to the shelf, accumulating dust, taken down and blown off whenever there is a free moment. Literacy and math are more important than food and water, a clean school, a safe and beautiful community. I love literacy and mathematics, don't get me wrong. My whole life has been dedicated to the power of literacy. However, there is something terribly wrong when we force a child who is experiencing PTSD and is hungry to sit down and read for an hour.

Tearing Down False Structures

This book is a sidestep from the traditional reading assigned to educators. It is one big gulp-like parenthesis towards creating a new space, and devoting time to the exploration of a new theory and practice for teacher agency for equity. This book is in response to observations and concrete situations that have alerted me to the fact that we have fallen into the great abyss of a segregated mind, and in doing so, obfuscate the real intention behind the role of teacher and our purpose in society.

At its core, this book challenges our norms, our assumptions and our use of language—including the very words that I have loved so dearly such as *equity, social justice, achievement, school, learning differences, diversity.* I have seen how these words have been coopted in order to maintain the status quo, and rather than encourage wisdom and critical thinking and freedom and democracy they have become barriers to innovation and Authentic Presence in the schools, in conferences and in education settings. These words are now so strategically placed as frames through which our goodness and our natural human desire to treat all human beings fairly and with dignity are exploited.

In this book, I will continue to ask enduring, philosophical and pedagogical questions—questions that I continue to ask myself on a daily basis. Questions like, how does your everyday practice and use of language communicate your thinking about who is responsible for poverty? I believe the willingness to ask ourselves deep philosophical (and ideological) questions about our role as teachers and the nature of the society we have created for ourselves through action is critical if we are to move towards equity in any authentic way. A fundamental part of this work is understanding that education discourse has

> The willingness to ask ourselves deep philosophical (and ideological) questions about our role as teachers and the nature of the society we have created for ourselves through action is critical if we are to move towards equity in any authentic way.

functioned as a cultural tool to maintain hierarchies in social and class relationships, extending well beyond the realm of discourse or ideology. Dominant ideologies and discourse continue to frame individuals and individual identities through *language*.[6] So, in order for us to reimagine a totally different future for our practice, for how we do schooling, for how we build a more human egalitarian society, we must challenge that which we hold most dear, including our words, all that aims to define us as human beings, as intellectuals, as teachers.

However, this is only the beginning.

Notes

1. Freire, P. (1970). *Pedagogy of the Oppressed. 30th Anniversary Edition,* 2003. New York: Continuum.
2. Wise, T. (2015). *Under the Influence: Shaming the Poor, Praising the Rich and Sacrificing the Future of America.* City Lights Books, p. 37.
3. Wise, T. (2015). *Under the Affluence: Shaming the Poor, Praising the Rich and Sacrificing the Future of America.* City Lights Open Media, p. 31.
4. Haslett, A. (2016). Donald Trump, shamer in chief. *The Nation*, October.
5. As quoted by Tim Wise (2015). *Under the Affluence: Shaming the Poor, Praising the Rich and Sacrificing the Future of America.* City Lights Open Media, p. 100.
6. Ansari, S. (2013). Deconstructing College-Readiness in an Urban Black Context: Ideology, Discourse, and Practices. Thesis, University of Illinois at Chicago.

2

Perspective

"Perhaps the hardest lesson for all of us to learn is that human identity is not settled but in motion, that reality is not fixed and solid but dynamic. We often act as if the future is going to be a lot like the present, only moreso, but the truth is that the future is unknown, of course, and also unknowable."

William Ayers, 2004, *Teaching Toward Freedom*[1]

I was born questioning. Critical inquiry is central to who I am and central to how I conduct myself in the world. Honest education praxis from my point of view is a constant cycle of reflection, application and theorizing. As a mindful scholar practitioner who comes from a heritage of poverty and oppression and who has always worked outside the Academy, I consider everyday practice and personal experience to be essential to authenticity, truth and agency in teaching and learning for equity.

In my experience, we do not separate the personal from the professional in education. Education is fundamentally about survival and if anyone tells you anything different, they are lying to you or living in denial. Education is about human development and the evolution of our species. These three things, survival, human development and the evolution of our species, make it impossible for us not take the business of education very personally. The level of personalization of the work increases when you have your own children and you begin to understand how the work of teaching and learning happens in the home and the impact of love and advocacy on the full nurturing of a child's curiosity and intellectual mind.

All of education is a life-work experience. Every moment of our existence, starting even before we are born, informs our understanding of survival, human development and evolution and by extension, each and every moment, each and every emotion, thought, sensation and experience impacts our understanding of the teaching and learning phenomena. Every situation in life is an opportunity to analyze, criticize and alter social, economic, cultural, technological and psychological structures and phenomena that have features of oppression, domination, exploitation, injustice and misery.[2]

Transforming Reality

The practice of teaching and learning is a transformative experience whether you are aware of it or not. All teaching and learning transforms our reality. Even the so-called "bad" educational experiences transform because in those moments of education failure, we create a hunger for something else, something better. Transformation happens when we challenge the way things are done and have always been done in order to differentiate our own thoughts and values from those of the community within which we work in order to develop authenticity.[3] Even when you think this type of learning is not happening, let me assure you that it is. Human beings are sponge-like organisms that never remain static. We are expertly designed to critique the world and transform the world through consciousness, all that which results from our everyday interaction with the world. Life is the laboratory for personal and collective consciousness and authenticity is indeed central to the process.

According to Edmund O'Sullivan, the founder of the Transformative Learning Center in Ontario, "Transformation involves a deep structural shift in the basic premises of thought, feelings and actions. It dramatically alters our way of being in the world. Such a shift involves our understanding of ourselves and our self-locations; our relationships with other humans and the natural world; our understanding of relations of power in the interlocking structures of class, race and gender; our body awareness, our visions of alternative approaches to living; and our sense of possibility for social justice, and peace and personal joy."[4] That is to say, every interaction, even interactions we hardly take notice of as learning experiences, are integral sources of personal and collective transformation.

Here is a simple example of an everyday transformation. While preparing for a presentation for teachers, I start a conversation with the custodial worker assigned to our room. He tells me that my type of work is important, but no matter how much we try to perfect the school and the teacher, nothing will ever change until we realize that a perfect school in the middle of an impoverished ghetto can never amount to anything. I look up from my neat binder and pile of handouts. The African-American man leans over with a squint in his left eye and asks, "What message are we giving a child when we invest in the school but neglect his parents and his community?" I think about this for a long time and I am transformed.

Scholar-practitioners move back and forth between theory and practice as they learn and apply new concepts and skills in their work and also in their lives.[5,6] Every interaction for the scholar-practitioner must become about learning and the willingness to apply the new learning to one's practice; including learning that we often disregard or devalue because of how we position people or label each other professionally. For example, what can we learn from the parent volunteer assigned to work in our classroom? In my experience, members of the school community such as parent volunteers or para-professionals who often live in the community are not considered as having any real "academic" value in the classroom. Teachers turn to them for help on issues of discipline or translation, but they do not consider them as colleagues who can share insights, practices or approaches to teaching and learning. We would never consider the school guard for

The full integration of the personal and the professional must exist if we want to transform our practice.

example as someone who might be able to alter our fundamental beliefs about teaching and learning. And yet the full integration of the personal and the professional must exist if we want to transform our practice.

Accepting Implicit Bias

In writing this book, I do not pretend to be neutral nor objective but rather, I accept bias—the natural bias of my own situation and context—in order to try to transcend it. The awareness of self and reality and interactions is a positive value in itself and should be present in research processes.[7] My own life as well as my craft as an educator, a researcher, a writer and a mother is always present in my search for truth in education for equity. According to Le Compte, bias always comes from two sources, personal experience and professional training. I cannot offer you mathematical explanations of my biases, only a desire to adhere to the highest form of disciplined honesty.[8] For this reason, I will share aspects of my life that have impacted my education philosophy and my work around teaching and learning for equity.

To start, I was a precocious child born into a family with a history of adversity. My grandmother was orphaned in a fire in Puerto Rico and raised by Catholic nuns. When she turned thirty, they put her on a boat to Brooklyn to work for a Jewish family in exchange for room, board, a meager salary and the promise of piano lessons. My grandmother, I was told, was a talented piano player. Unfortunately, upon her arrival to Brooklyn, she learned the work arrangement did not include access to the piano.

We were an immigrant family struggling to survive in New York City. At the time my grandmother arrived (circa 1939), New York City was one of the main recipients of immigrants from Puerto Rico.[9] Expectations for success in America for Puerto Ricans were dismal. In 1935, for example, the New York State Chamber of Commerce's Special Committee on Immigration and

Naturalization commissioned a study on the intelligence (IQ) of 240 Puerto Rican schoolchildren in East Harlem that stigmatized them as being "intellectually deficient."[10] Although many argued that these results were due to the children's lack of familiarity of the English language, reactions to Puerto Rican immigration became toxic. Puerto Ricans, who were often poor, identified as "mixed race," and lacked language and literacy skills, had a difficult time in America, and still do. Fortunately, my grandmother, like many "voiceless" Puerto Ricans, was disciplined, filled with faith and advocated for her children in clever ways that made a difference.

In spite of adversity, both my parents performed relatively well in school (my mother attended Catholic schools and my father public). Both my parents eventually went on to college (my father first, my mother much later on) and thereby gained access to what they called the "middle class." For them the middle class meant leaving government housing or "the projects" and being able to mortgage a house in a nice neighborhood. My father went on to become an engineer and at the age of fifty, my mother finally settled into her life's purpose and career as a social worker. Although they eventually divorced, both my parents believed that education was a prerequisite for social mobility. Through my mother's second marriage to an African American with a career in law enforcement who was deeply involved in the Harlem arts community, I learned about the black experience and the power of community building.

It is an understatement to say that throughout my youth, I was exposed to all walks of life. I interacted with folks who were dirt poor, lived on welfare or worked menial labor jobs and others who were highly educated, middle and upper class. Growing up in the northwest section of the Bronx afforded me friends from all races and ethnic backgrounds, although I would say the neighborhood was still predominantly Jewish at the time. This worked in my favor in many ways. One, I learned to appreciate the true power of the integrated schooling experience and two, Jews had a reputation for commitment to education. They also had economic stability. Having Jewish friends and Jewish teachers reinforced my mother's teaching at home that only an intellectual life was worth living.

My sixth grade teacher, Mrs. Morrison, wrote in my graduation signature book, "Who is going to ask me why, when, what, where and how?" When I was tracked to attend a less desirable school in spite of my Jewish friends getting into the better one, Mrs. Morrison offered to be my "aunt" and advocate for me. As it turns out, I didn't need a Jewish aunt since my Latino mother took my hand and walked me over to the good school office and demanded I be admitted. When they told her that any discrepancy was a result of some students wanting to learn Hebrew (which was only offered at that one school), my mother reassured them that Hebrew was her daughter's lifelong passion. They accepted me into the school and assigned me to Spanish for beginners. This was my legacy of agency.

I was a smart kid. I got accepted to Bronx High School of Science and Phillips Exeter Academy. I transferred to Exeter and did well academically, but I struggled socially and emotionally. Against my parents' wishes after one year at the elite boarding school, I came home, graduated from a small, Catholic school and eventually got accepted to New York University's School of Education. Little did I know that my unique schooling experiences would prepare me for my future. As most of you are aware, more often than not, schools that serve Latino immigrant youth fail to become vehicles through which their dreams and aspirations can be fulfilled.[11] Even before I became a teacher, I naturally sought out answers to this dilemma. What are those essential factors needed to develop and inspire children to become life-long learners and fulfill their dreams?

When I became a teacher and later a professional development specialist, I was often the only woman of Puerto Rican decent. Sadly, my experience is similar to how Sonia Nieto describes her experiences as a Puerto Rican educator when she first started teaching in the 1960s at Ocean Hill-Brownsville community school in Brooklyn. In her book *Brooklyn Dreams*, she writes, "Acquainted only with Puerto Ricans who lived in poverty, colleagues appeared surprised to meet an educated and middle class Puerto Rican, one returning from Spain and with a Master's Degree."[12] The more I evolved as an educator, the more I became aware of the fact that I was considered an outlier.

There is a dearth of Latino educators overall and even fewer from Puerto Rican descent. Even books, articles and reports on education about Puerto Ricans were rarely written by Puerto Ricans.[13] It is no wonder that people have internalized Latinos as being simply poor, uneducated, lacking in good English language skills and lacking in the necessary mindset to engage intellectually. Even to this day, when you turn on the television, Latino women are depicted as housekeepers, nannies or portrayed as sex symbols.

The school environment became the laboratory for my thinking and conscientization as a critical educator. Conscientization, according to Freire, is the in-depth awareness of the socio-political and cultural dynamics of the world that includes a deep understanding of power relationships. Like many Latinos and African Americans before me, regardless of the quality of my work, I experienced disparaging comments, prejudice and acts of discrimination along the way. A colleague in a wealthy school district told me to wear lipstick so the students wouldn't mistake me for the help, for example. In the same district students mocked an assignment requiring that they interview a Spanish speaker by asking, you really want us to mix with the servants? I also witnessed discrimination and poor decision-making. I witnessed how decisions were being made about Latino students because of biases and assumptions about their intellectual capacity or the level of investment of their family. The level of language acquisition in English is still often equated to intelligence. Afro-Latinos have it particularly hard because they deal with language marginalization as well as racism. By engaging in schools and professional conversations across all of these diverse learning spaces, I have learned just how often our upbringing, personal experience and bias translate to real decision-making.

My doctoral research introduced me to Paulo Freire's work. I couldn't understand why throughout all my years of schooling I had not been exposed to Freire. He gave me a language and validated my thinking. I began to understand Academia as a protected class reserved for those who have access to specific set of circumstances. It is shameful how in the education community we continue to create mystery and prestige around the notion of scholarship. If only every parent and child knew that "research" and "scholarship" are just code words for curiosity and access rather than some genetic predisposition.

Shortly after I graduated from an unconventional doctoral program, I found myself struggling to survive. That year coincided with the widespread collapse of our economy in 2008. Like thousands of Americans, I lost my house, savings and was left unemployed for long periods of time. During that time, I witnessed how the bipartisan neoliberal agenda to privatize public schools with the proliferation of charter schools as one of their primary tools began to wipe out our national regard for "public" school. This was an attack on our shared sense of social responsibility and any critical consciousness that understood public schools as being a fundamental institution within a healthy democracy. I witnessed mass school closings and vicious attacks on the teaching profession. Educators were being displaced and traumatized, losing jobs and trying to decipher the rules of this new market-driven education game. Dana Goldstein wrote, "To many American teachers, the last decade of value added school reform felt like something imposed upon them from outside and above—by politicians with little expertise in teaching and learning, by corporate philanthropists who long to remake education into the mold of the business world, and by economists who see teaching as less of an art than as science."[14] These were confusing years. They were probably just as startling as the upheaval of the desegregation of schools in the sixties coupled with President Johnson's ambitious efforts to move ahead his War on Poverty. Johnson's policies, accountability efforts and the authorization of a National Teacher Corp (which recruited elite, young college students to teach) also led to the disproportionate loss of teaching jobs held by veteran African-American teachers.[15]

Feeling both isolated and inundated with news about the greatest attack on the teaching profession, my conscientization shifted from the laboratory of the school to the laboratory of my mind. It was not the first time I relied on my spirit, but this time I took full notice of it. All the times that I had watched my grandmother pray (a daily ritual) made more sense to me. She had survived so much worse, raising four kids with limited English. There was an emerging sense of Spirit Consciousness as a pathway to navigate transformation and heal the mourning of our beloved teaching profession. During this time, I spent a lot of time reflecting on my own personal experiences and through writing I began to reach out to educators over the Internet. Within a short time, a very small network of hope and community emerged around me and I began to get a deeper sense of the fragility of teacher agency. I wondered: How does one make a difference in the world, or devote one's life to the service of others, when you are unemployed or worried about losing a house and paying the bills? Like a phenomenologist, I began to jot down details of my own life as a map to better understanding what was happening to the world around me. I became intrigued not so much with identity politics, which had dominated my thinking previously, but with the profound inner and spiritual life of a teacher, a person who by profession will always be at the epicenter of any social upheaval.

So while reformers were busy dismantling and restructuring public education piece by piece, damaging poor communities and communities of color the most, I began to wonder, how do we really expect teachers to behave? Do we really expect them to advocate for the rights of poor black and brown children while living in a climate of fear and uncertainty? How do these brutal attacks on the teaching profession impact the social-emotional and spiritual well-being of teachers? How is our inner landscape changing, our sense of agency and empowerment, and how are teachers holding onto a sense of self-worth and value in a fast-changing, data-driven world that seems to be creating strife rather than unifying the country?

As I fumbled through the litany of coded questions that characterized many of the phone interviews I engaged in at the time looking for a job, I began to understand shame and cowardice. Why are you forcing me to choose this new model of education reform that I don't believe in that I know will be at the expense of what Delpit aptly referred to as, "other people's children?" Later, much later, I read about a teacher by the name of Gus Morales who spoke out against data walls and high-stakes testing and got fired for it, and then demanded that teachers have courage and honor under what he called "the Educratic Oath." "Do no harm! Do no harm!" he said.

Where does one find the courage to "do no harm"?

Validating Our Experiences

These personal lived experiences, especially those that jettison us out of our comfort zone, have the power to reveal to us what is important and what it means to live an authentic life. These life lessons sometimes carry greater weight than years of study. Over the last decade, I have found that learning to validate, share and honor the developments that emerge out of the realm of one's personal space is extremely important, especially for teachers. We are living in a time in which the news and much of our public space has become one big spectacle. We are bombarded with rhetoric that dominates most of our air space, and threatens our freedom to think independently. Throughout this book you will see how a critical role of a conscientious educator is learning how to combat this barrage of false information and lies and get quiet, tuning into and validating one's most inner, personal space. This is particularly important and challenging for women who work in the home, the poor, the oppressed, people of color who experience chronic stress from racism and people who belong to indigenous and tribal communities who have a long history of marginalization. These groups, of which I am a part, are often subjects and objectified, but rarely are we made central to the discovery of truth and knowledge, which requires that we give reverence to our personal space.

When we experience chaos or are pushed out of our norm, we are accessing different parts of our mind and expanding consciousness. In precisely these moments of deeply

> Learning to validate, share and honor the developments that emerge out of the realm of one's personal space is extremely important, especially for teachers.

personal human dilemma, we enter the territory of universal wisdom—this is where courage is born. Each individual is in the position to inform and shape, through the validation of their personal experiences, the greatest social movement of our time. In accepting this, each of us becomes an instrument through which our collective culture evolves.

Reflection Questions

1. What does it mean to engage in Mindful Inquiry as a scholar-practitioner?
2. How do your personal and professional relationships inform your understanding of equity?
3. How have attacks on the teaching profession, "value added" reforms and/or the current political landscape impacted your social, emotional and spiritual well-being?

Notes

1. Ayers, W. (2004). *Teaching Toward Freedom*. Boston: Beacon Press.
2. Bentz, V.M. & Shapiro, J.J. (1998). *Mindful Inquiry in Social Research*. Thousand Oaks, London, California: Sage Publications, International Educational and Professional Publishers, p. 146.
3. Cranton, P. & Carusetta, E. (2004). Perspectives on authenticity in teaching. *Adult Education Quarterly*, Vol. 55, No. 1, pp. 5–22.
4. O'Sullivan, E. (2005). Emancitory hope: Transformative learning and the "strange attractors." In Miller, J.P. et al. (eds.), *Holistic Learning and Spirituality in Education: Breaking New Ground*. State University of New York Press, p. 76.
5. Bentz, V.M. & Shapiro, J.J. (1998). *Mindful Inquiry in Social Research*. Thousand Oaks, London, California: Sage Publications, International Educational and Professional Publishers, p. 146.
6. Schon, D. A. (1983). *The Reflective Practitioner: How Professionals Think in Action*. New York: Basic Books.
7. Bentz, V.M. & Shapiro, J.J. (1998). *Mindful Inquiry in Social Research*. Thousand Oaks, London, California: Sage Publications, International Educational and Professional Publishers, p. 146.

8. LeCompte, M. (1987) Bias in the biography: Bias and subjectivity in ethnographic research. *Anthropology and Education Quarterly*, Vol. 18., No. 1, pp. 43–52.

9. Chenault, L.R. (1970). *The Puerto Rican Migrant in New York City*. Russel & Russel, p. 57.

10. Sanchez Korrol, V. (2014). *The Story of US Puerto Ricans Part Six*. Center for Puerto Rican Studies, Hunter College. Available online at: http://humanvarieties.org/2014/03/13/hvgiq-puerto-rico-2/#section2b

11. Noguera, P.A. (2006). Latino youth: Immigration, education and the future. *Latino Studies*, Vol. 4, pp. 313–320.

12. Nieto, S. (2015). *Brooklyn Dreams: My Life in Public Education*. Cambridge, MA: Harvard Education Press, p. 132.

13. Ibid., p. 174.

14. Goldstein, D. (2014). *The Teacher Wars: A History of America's Most Embattled Profession*. New York: Doubleday.

15. Ibid., p. 122.

3

Poverty Consciousness

Equity is about the distribution of resources. Equity or inequity is a direct result of the choices we make. It is not a discussion about laziness or gaps to fill in. It is simply determining how much value we place on a human being.

I first learned about poverty from my parents and then from my husband's family, who live in a working-class town on the southern coast of Spain. I come from a long line of very poor people. I have been thinking about what it means to be poor for most of my life.

I was born into a poor Puerto Rican immigrant family, which is worse than just being born poor. Unlike the Irish, Italians and Jewish immigrants who would gradually be accepted as full-fledged [white] Americans,[1,2] Puerto Ricans like my family, in spite of their American citizenship, would never be accepted as American nor experience similar upward social mobility.[3]

The act of reflecting on and having an awareness of the status of my birth as a demographic, as a statistic, as having a heritage of poverty, is poverty consciousness. No matter what I do in life, whether I end up accomplished or not, I will always be a part of this class of people called others. I have taken ownership, finally, of this perspective of life that uniquely comes with a sense of "otherness." Poverty consciousness is not about identity nor is it about culture. It is an awareness of the value we attach to the totality of a human being in relation to others within the socio-cultural political dynamics of our world. This awareness is constantly evolving as is the relative value we place on some and the criteria we use to come to such values. Although there are fluctuating circumstances similar to the stock market (acquiring a degree, for example, may increase the total value of your existence), there are also certain "fixed" values we attach to race or even gender. The awareness of one's own total human value may change depending on circumstances related to context. Where do you live? With who are you standing? For how long have you been unemployed, exactly? Being exposed to the precariousness of personal safety or financial stability, not only for you but also for your loved ones, impacts your level of poverty consciousness.

Being unable to resist the examination of poverty consciousness has been a cross and a blessing. In the last decade in particular I have become extremely sensitive to the human suffering that occurs when you do not know how you are going to make ends meet, pay for basic necessities, or be able to raise your children with dignity. Poverty consciousness has helped me makes sense of myself, and begin the process of defining for myself what it means to live with integrity as a human being and what is important in spite of the economic conditions I may have to experience in this world. Poverty consciousness has been essential in my understanding and development of agency for equity.

I am sometimes in the midst of people with money. Sometimes they ask and sometimes they don't ask the question, what do you think about this or that? Sometimes I think they don't want to assume I know what it is to be poor. Or maybe they don't want to personalize our work. It makes people feel uncomfortable to humanize the object of a discussion as if when we are talking about equity, we are engaging in objective science and that putting real faces to the work (like mine) or real stories, we may lose hold of our ability to learn. We might even feel obligated.

I don't have some unique insight that will help politicians unpack the conundrum of education failure for poor people, but I do think some things must be said in response to some of the vileness I hear and feel, and even absorb myself in response to our political narrative that idolizes wealth.

We All Want the Same Things

We all want goodness for our children. It is part of the human condition to love our children and to strive for a better life, passing on lessons learned from one generation to the next. This is human instinct. We all have dreams. Contrary to what many say about "other, less than" groups, we want to find purpose in life, to find meaningful work and be in the position to provide a decent life for our offspring and ourselves. In this way, we are simply human. In this way, we distinguish ourselves from animals. For this reason, whenever I hear someone say that a child, a family or a group does not value education, I don't respond. I just wait and think—how is it possible that a person can arrive at such a conclusion? How is it that they do not see this child, this family or this group as human beings?

As human beings, we seek fulfillment in loving, protecting and nurturing our children to become well-rounded, compassionate and caring adults. This can be pretty hard to do living in a racist, hegemonic society. People pray hard and plant seeds in children hoping that maybe it will be a little easier to live in the future. We are hopeful that as part of the human race, we will eventually evolve into more caring, compassionate, egalitarian people. In Spanish, the word for hope is *esperanza*. The root, *espera*, means to wait.

For those of us who can afford to manage it, we cultivate in our children a value for society and education through good manners, literacy and a respectful career path so that in the very least, we have done our part in pushing forward our young. For some Latinos living in America, that may mean acculturation, becoming a little more like the dominant group, "Anglos," who continue to be considered the authorities on what it means to be successful and intelligent in life. Some may develop a proclivity for suburbia—anything that we attach to normative notions of American success and that is set far away from urban poverty and the clumsy awkwardness of being a poor, Latino immigrant with an accent. Many voted Republican in this past election. Some measure each step in life as a choice towards something higher or lower, starting with one's original identity. Please don't mistake this behavior for lack of pride—this is simply survival and understanding the rules of monopoly. We love ourselves that much, to give up that which may hold us back for the betterment of our children.

Some of us don't manage oppression well. Shame, embarrassment and fear are prevalent in segregated, poor communities. No one wants to clean toilets for a living, become addicted to drugs, prostitute oneself, live in filth or get arrested. But it happens every day and understanding this as part of poverty consciousness is important—that is, knowing that survival is an everyday battle for some and even when you work hard, too hard sometimes, it doesn't always mean you are going to get out and if you do, there is the fear that you will lose it all in an instant. Some of us live multiple lives like imposters, hiding the complexity of inheriting a poor beginning, loving our parents but wanting to flee in order to preserve oneself.

What Are Children Learning from Us?

What do our children learn about the world watching their parents navigate their existence through a lens of poverty consciousness? They learn the dance between the inner and outer world, the ongoing act of wanting and becoming simultaneously and never having the luxury to stop and rest and just be. They learn life can be utterly exhausting and that there is suffering. They learn to accept complex, often contradictory feelings about success and achievement because if one person can do it, does it mean you were just lucky? Or does it mean you are smarter, braver, stronger and born with certain qualities and characteristics deemed by the mainstream as being worthy? It is not fear of being these things, contrary to what many think. Smarter *is* cool, but it distinguishes oneself from the majority and that is a lonely place to be, especially if you are leaving your brothers, sisters or parents behind.

What responsibility do we owe our children who do well but come from poorer communities? If you stay behind you are exposing yourself and your children to lower-quality services, fewer resources, violence, confusion, segregated schools, and so on. What is needed for children to invest in their own community when they grow up? This is a question worth our time. What structural and systemic elements must be in place so that they are more likely to take ownership of community businesses and property? How can we guarantee that their hard work and success can provide them with a higher standard of living within their own community? These are all questions that matter.

There is failure because we are not all superheroes. No one who has children wants them to fail, although generations of pain and suffering have in some cases created abuse, neglect and apathy. Still, in my experience, contrary to what we hear about poor people, I have found that most poor people love deeply and fight hard to make a better experience for their young. Most poor people care about each other and support each other in spite of the abuse they endure on a day-to-day basis from the outside world. Poor people are some of the most faithful and hopeful people in the world. Some immerse themselves in religion for this reason.

Poor people want to see their children flourish, to reach the sky, to be free, to be recognized for the greatness inside them, to have choices, to discover the world—even if that means self-sacrifice or teaching them to choose things in life that are far removed from who they are at birth. This is the divine expectation of all human life. If you are struggling or destitute or enslaved, if you are poor or treated as "other, less than otherness," then your instinct may be to preserve your dignity by hiding this pain. Some parents who are poor and have suffered a life of abuse may choose to hide their suffering from their children because they want them to have something better and more, something good, and they want them not to see such darkness. Do you understand what I'm saying here? This is what I mean by embarrassment, shame and fear.

We live in a society where abject poverty and filthy wealth live side by side and we tell ourselves this state of reality is okay. We tell ourselves we are victims to the natural order of things, that we are not creating this reality but rather we are innocent bystanders of a biological sorting and sifting.

A Teacher's Silent Struggle

Teachers in particular are confronted daily with thoughts of contempt, embarrassment, shame and fear. They experience these emotions because contrary to misleading thoughts of a segregated mind, we are all living the impact of the precarious conditions we face in society and as human beings; we absorb the thoughts and emotions associated with such experiences. As such, we are all equally filled with disdain, shame, embarrassment and fear— not only for the future of the children in our care, but for our own well-being, regardless if we have been positioned by our role in society as oppressor, privileged or a pedagogical authority. We do what we need to do to survive. We are a part of the ugliness and even though we tell ourselves that we are working overtime to do our best, every teacher feels dangerously close to falling into that pit of despair. Rationalizing the suffering and poverty for some people in society is part of our national identity, but it does not have to be a fixed part of the future. A segregated mind is not natural; we are built for wholeness and integral consciousness. Racism and poverty are not natural. It is how we have been taught, to sort and sift identities and the realities we associate with them, in order that some prosper at the expense of the suffering of others. We have a choice.

> Rationalizing the suffering and poverty for some people in society is part of our national identity, but it does not have to be a fixed part of the future.

Some of us may continue to choose to live in a bubble. We tell ourselves, haven't I done enough?

It becomes easier and easier to walk away. Or not.

Reflection Questions

1. What is your understanding of poverty consciousness?
2. How does your professional learning community explain poverty and/or characterize the culture of poverty as it relates to learning?
3. Do you believe that it's possible that we can arrive at a more egalitarian society in the United States? Why or why not?

Notes

1. Roediger, D. (1991). *The Wages of Whiteness*. New York: Verso Press.
2. Brodkin, K. (1999). *How Jews Became White Folk and What That Says About Race in America*. New Brunswick, NJ: Rutgers University Press.
3. Noguera, P.A. (2006). Latino Youth: Immigration, Education and the Future. *Latino Studies*, Vol. 4, pp. 313-320.

4

Racism

It is very common for teachers to either think that race and racism do not really have much meaning in today's world because we are all so beyond caring about it or that since talking about race and racism has been so accepted in academic settings, we don't need to acknowledge the gaps between theory and practice amongst educators.[1] I have come to find in my practice that regardless of the heinous crimes we are witnessing every day against black people rooted in gun violence, racial profiling and abuses in law enforcement, these alarming social issues, issues about our dehumanization of black people, issues that are rooted in a history of slavery, decades of segregation and high poverty, don't typically come up in conversations with teachers when we are talking about teacher effectiveness. This is the case even as we learn about research that uncovers racial bias, such as Rachel Fish's new study out of New York University. Students of different racial and ethnic backgrounds are still perceived and treated differently and this bias does impact student placement in gifted programs and special education.[2]

I have noticed increasingly that during high-level conversations, race and racism are not mentioned. Race consciousness on the part of either whites or blacks is marginalized as beyond the good sense of enlightened people and I do believe that there is this false assumption that to have race consciousness is to become racist.[3] This is the "I don't see color" rationale we still hear often in education circles.

When my children came home from school after the Eric Garner incident (we live in New York City), I was told that not one teacher broached the subject and the school day continued on just like any other day. Oddly, the day after, I had a professional development engagement in the Bronx. A member of my team raised the question whether or not we should address the incident. Ultimately, it was decided that we would be remiss if we ignored the opportunity to talk about racism, especially as we were in the unique position to support teachers going back to schools where students might be noticeably upset. Although I was glad the Gardner killing would not be ignored, I deeply regret that while I was the only "woman of color" on our team with an academic background in social justice pedagogy, there was lengthy deliberation amongst my white colleagues (in leadership positions) about whether I should be involved in the planning process or be allowed to deliver the message at all.

The Impact of Racism

We can't talk about teaching and learning for equity without considering the impact of racism on our collective consciousness. Poverty and racism are two different things, although sadly, they often do go hand-in-hand in our country. I have noticed in education circles how we speak of race and poverty interchangeably, like when educators refer to high-poverty schools, urban schools or low-performing schools, for example; what they are also saying is that we are talking about black and brown children. Not all black and brown kids are poor and not all white kids are well-off or educated in private schools, yet in education circles I have observed this blending of race and class in our everyday use of language that muddles conversations and plays with our perception of reality. Who are we talking about exactly and what are the conditions we are aiming to address? Ambiguity around race and poverty allows educators to conveniently pivot away from the hard conversations. Nonetheless, in more recent years, discourse about race and racism in particular have been much more accepted into academic settings even though black people and people of color have been to some extent psychologically terrorized by the bizarre gaps between theory and practice.[4]

Racism is considerably the most powerful weapon ever designed. Similarly to terrorism it cannot be contained nor can it be easily eradicated. This is because it is a parasitic ideology that thrives off the human survival instinct. Racism is so intricately woven into the fabric of our existence that we don't even know where it begins or ends nor are most of us ever fully aware of the countless ways it manifests itself in ourselves and in the everyday workings of society.

One thing that is important to understand is that we have all inherited the impact of racism; it is a strand on our individual and collective DNA. That means that each individual manifests the effects of racism in different ways, as well as each community. The impact of racism has festered in us for hundreds and hundreds of years; the human suffering, guilt and confusion that result from racist ideology are now a part of our collective consciousness.

At its core, racist ideology aims to divide and sort humanity into rival clans so that there is no chance for unity, love and the sharing of earth's resources. It is rooted in two fundamental assumptions or beliefs: survival of the fittest and scarcity. The first refers to the notion that the nature of human beings is to fight to survive and those who survive do so because they are stronger and/or more intelligent. The second refers to the belief that there are limited resources available to human beings and survival requires competition for access to those scarce resources. Both of these speak to this idea of human being as predator. Racist ideology teaches that some clans, some human beings, are inherently superior or inferior and that is why they survive, have accumulated power or wealth and have dominated the world. This notion of superiority and inferiority genetically inherited at birth is the basis for decision-making, the abuse of power and, in many ways, continues to impact all types of policies that ensure that one clan will always survive over another.

Racism is taught, learned, nurtured and perpetuated in every aspect of society. For it to work, it must be so impregnated in the mind, body and spirit of people that the people themselves act on racist ideology even if that means working against oneself. Racist ideology over time becomes the norm and dominant culture. It is a fine layer or film that colors your entire worldview and how you interpret every event, every happening. As racism thrives on fear for survival, fear is systematically attached to specific races. Hate is an extension of fear, so fear and hate are the key drivers of racist ideology.

Manifestations of Racism

At this point in our human evolution, we cannot label racism "unconscious bias." We have certainly evolved enough so that we all have an awareness of the impact and existence of racism historically and in present-day reality and even globally. However, the subtle ways that racism manifests itself in people and systems are still so layered and complex, it makes it possible for a person to understand racist ideology but behave in racist ways in some area of their lives. This is what bell hooks talks about when she describes "the bizarre gaps between theory and practice." She writes, "a well meaning liberal white female professor might write a useful book on the intersections of race and gender yet continue to allow racist biases to shape the manner in which she responds personally to women of color."[5] In my experience, this schism between theory and practice is prevalent in contemporary education circles where there is great passion for liberal intellectualism, social justice and notions of equity which serves well in raising money for the organization but who in every day practice embody racist ideology. An example of this is my experience working with privileged white women who self identify as liberal and social justice minded holding leadership positions in organizations that are in service of "all" students, the poor or marginalized peoples but who pass over highly qualified people of color for decision-making, promotions or opportunities for professional development internally. Many people advocate for equity and social justice and make a fine living off it, but in every day practice hoard access to real political power, resources and information that systematically keeps people of color and poor people in subordinate positions. The rationale is that gaining access to leadership and political power is because of specific qualifications and credentials rather than institutionalized racism.

Some people consider racism a disease. Others consider it an evil. Racism at its core is the absolute opposite of love because it directly aims its attack at the fundamental core of the human spirit. That is why I believe that any education theory or practice in a system where injustice persists that does not pay attention to the dynamics of the spirit is indicative of hegemonic ideology. An African-American teacher educator and colleague, Lybroan James, explained this best. He said, "black people would have never survived slavery, attempts at genocide, and other crimes against their humanity if it not were for them being a fundamentally spiritual people. If teachers can't relate to students of color in a humane and holistic way and use what they know about social and emotional learning as a way to lead them to a higher consciousness and inclusiveness of culture, then they are not going to be successful."

> Racism at its core is the absolute opposite of love because it directly aims its attack at the fundamental core of the human spirit.

Racism in Education

Most people in education do not like to talk deeply about the impact of race and racism on our work. It is easier to stick with the technical aspects of skill development because we feel in control. It is also because educators don't want to face our ugly history of slavery in which blacks were not allowed to learn to read and our treatment of the Native American populations in boarding schools, followed by a long history of segregation (that persists today). Talking deeply about the impact of racism in education is very painful. What you hear often from white educators is that they are so tired of talking about it. In 2003, bell hooks wrote a book called *Teaching Community*. As referenced earlier, she wrote, "Groups where white folks are in the majority often insist that race and racism does not really have much meaning in today's world because we are so beyond caring about it." She continues on to say, "I ask them why then do they have so much fear about speaking their minds. Their fear, their censoring silence, is indicative of the loaded meaning race and racism still have in our society." People argue that by addressing racism, we are being divisive. I think these are all ways to deflect our spiritual fatigue and powerlessness because really, how can talking about racism as a form of activism be more divisive than the cancer itself?

> If teachers feel powerless to address the deeper, broader, more important issues of racism in our society like desegregating schools and eradicating the inequitable funding of schools, issues that would have a real impact, then we lose agency for equity.

Agency and powerlessness are opposites. If teachers feel powerless to address the deeper, broader, more important issues of racism in our society like desegregating schools and eradicating the inequitable funding of schools, issues that would have a real impact, then we lose agency for equity. If anti-racist work in education remains at the superficial level, like say, learning how to appreciate each other's cultural differences and perspectives or adding more brown faces to the company directory, then we are going to feel powerless and lose agency for equity.

In my career, I have had to sit amidst wonderful, bright, well-intentioned educators with impressive degrees who look forlorn and perplexed when the issue of race comes up. They turn to me and communicate how complex the topic is and sometimes they look to me for answers even though they know I am in no position of authority to do anything. They look to me for answers to the same questions they have been asking other people of color without giving them any chance at real political power for hundreds of years. Meanwhile, other topics in education seem to move along rather smoothly. Somehow, racism is always cast into this special other dimension called ineptitude.

Racism is one of those simple truths. We have always known what to do, yet accepting the horrific impact of racism on families, children and teachers as one of our collective truths requires that we take action and sadly, as time goes by, I find that more and more educators choose to repress any inclination to embrace the truth and work together to find a restorative solution.

Reflection Questions

1. What is your understanding of racist ideology? What type of thoughts do you have about various racialized groups, including your own?
2. How might racist ideologies have impacted your professional relationships and your organization's approach to addressing equity in education?
3. How comfortable are you in addressing issues of race and racism with colleagues? How do the dynamics of race change depending on who is in the room?
4. How have recent social and political events shaped your thinking about race and racism in this country? How might this influence our work in education for equity?

Notes

1. hooks, b (2003). *Teaching Community*. New York: Routledge, pp. 28–29.
2. Rankin, K. (2016). STUDY: Race Impacts Student Referrals for Gifted, Special Education. *Colorlines*. Available online at: http://www.colorlines.com/articles/study-race-impacts-student-referrals-gifted-special-education Study author Rachel Fish: "This subjectivity has implications for inequalities in education by race and ethnicity."

3. Gatimu, M.W. (2009) Undermining critical consciousness unconsciously: Restoring hope in the multicultural education Idea. *Journal of Educational Change*, Vol. 10, No. 1, pp. 47–61.
4. hooks, b (2003) *Teaching Community*. New York: Routledge, p. 26.
5. Ibid., p. 27.

5

Conscientious Engagement

"I have no technical terminology and no knowledge of academic discipline. This isn't boasting, nor is it an apology; it is just a means of reminding myself of what my reality has been and what I am. At this point it might be useful for us to ask ourselves a few questions: what is this act, what is this scene in which the action is taking place, what is this agency and what is its purpose?"

Ralph Ellison, *Lecture to Teachers*, 1963[1]

I have had many interesting conversations with teachers and teacher educators about the general malaise around teacher agency and equity over the course of my career. Conversations of this nature often take place immediately after a professional learning session surrounded by the hustle and bustle of teachers anxious to return to the demands of their school buildings. However, the deeper, more reflective conversations about the teaching profession and equity in particular typically take place in the safe space of a private, one-on-one. In recent years, I have noticed how these conversations about agency and equity have taken on a more urgent, somewhat clandestine quality. Teacher agency in its simplest terms is a teacher's belief in him or herself as someone who can make a difference in the world that *includes and extends beyond* the classroom or school context. I would also add that teacher agency involves a sense of empowerment and a feeling of control over important decisions at it relates to the education of students.

For 200 years, the American public has asked teachers to close troubling gaps. Early in our history it was between Catholics and Protestants; then it was between new immigrants and the American mainstream, blacks and white and poor and rich.[2] And yet, with the rise of inequality, increasing poverty, segregated schools and communities, an ideologically and politically divided country and friction over the new expectations of market-driven curriculum and instruction policies, teachers are right to question just how is it that a teacher is supposed to accomplish this? Even more importantly, teachers are beginning to challenge our national fixation on "closing gaps" as the primary work of teaching for equity. There is mounting evidence that such an extreme focus on gaps has either fueled the problem or in the very least, acted as a distraction that has allowed larger inequities to persist.[3] It is important to ask ourselves, what does our current approach to teaching for equity say about who is ultimately to blame for school failure and social inequality and how does that impact a teacher's sense of agency?

How Teachers Are Becoming Jaded

In a conversation with Dr. Rewa Chisholm, African-American in-service teacher educator with 22 years of education experience, she described the uncertainty around teacher agency for equity like this: "Most teachers go into the field thinking they are going to make a difference in the world. However, after a short time, they become jaded. Society's view on what it means to be a teacher becomes a dark cloud over their head. When teachers see what is actually going on in urban communities, in particular, they lose confidence in their ability to have any impact at all. The kids in poverty and the things they are dealing with, like hunger, coming to school without appropriate clothing, coming to school after witnessing a shootout, parents fighting with each other, etc.—and then, when they are confronted with the prevailing negative attitude towards education, it chips away at the rock. Not understanding the social-emotional needs of kids is our greatest barrier. If we figure out how to address the social-emotional needs of children, and prioritize that in policy, giving teachers time to understand what that looks like, then teachers might feel more empowered."

Over the 25-year period from 1987 to 2012, the minority share of the American teaching force—including Black, Hispanic, Asian and Pacific Islander, American Indian and multiracial teachers—has grown slightly from 12 percent to 17 percent while minority students now account for more than half of all public school students.[4] This means that while teachers in public schools are still predominantly white (and female), the majority of students are identified as "students of color." In many schools, the entire student population is diverse while the teacher demographic shifts slightly, accounting for the fact that minority teachers are often concentrated in high-minority, high-poverty schools. These statistics however do not refer to the socio-economic status of teachers, which is certainly important as we consider the type of "culture shock" teachers readily experience in a socio-economically segregated society.

"Young white teachers walk into these schools and they are stunned," Rewa says. "Educators of color who do not come from poverty are equally stunned at what they see and their life becomes a series of choices. Equity and professional expectations are constantly pitted against each other. I have noticed that many teachers learn that kids are not the problem—it's what people are doing to these kids that are causing a problem. This includes parent neglect, an often broken community, a system that does not prioritize social-emotional learning, health and safety—all of these things make a teacher's job hard."

Those who support teachers in the field are well aware that new teachers are quickly confronted with the reality that they may not be fully equipped to handle the socio-economic culture they encounter in schools and this we know impacts a teacher's ability to adequately assess and attend to the wide range of learning needs. This compounded with high-stakes testing and expectations to close "gaps" becomes a troubling mix. There have been numerous occasions over the last decade where I have worked with and/or coached teachers (of all races and socio-economic backgrounds) who become frantic as they prepare for a formal observation or evaluation. Not only do they worry how their students will behave and perform in front of a discerning guest, they also know that the standardized test scores will be added as evidence of their effectiveness.

"It is very likely that after a teacher does everything the district tells them to do, they may not see a positive result as evidenced by standardized test scores, so then teachers feel even more disempowered," Rewa explains. "They begin to question the overall approach. They begin to question whether expectations are realistic. Many children are so behind that it's a game of constant catch-up. You lose a sense of agency when you are not prepared with a realistic plan to move children forward in their learning regardless of the circumstances."

Pressure to Close "Achievement Gaps"

This dynamic can make a teacher feel insecure and inadequate or, alternatively, defensive and self-justifying. Such a laser-like focus on closing the achievement gap, *as evidenced by evaluations and test scores*, can in fact motivate teachers to deflect away from reflecting on their teaching practice and try to find blame in students and families. The desire to protect oneself professionally as a form of survival can explain why some teachers might want to get challenging students such as students with "special needs," out of their classrooms.

That recent study that I mentioned earlier that came out of New York University by Rachel Fish indicated that racial bias continues to impact whether a student is placed in special education or in gifted and talented programs.[5] Research has shown the disproportionate number of African-American boys, for example, in special education classes and gifted and talented programs composed of majority white students. Racial bias naturally spills over into school choice. One white, Jewish, New York teacher explained, "Parents don't want to send their children to schools where there are students of color, even if they are told the school is doing well. It's all about race perception." As a professional development specialist, I know how much we inundate teachers with research on race and class and its impact on student performance, but we do a very poor job in framing the data correctly so teachers can put data into the socio-cultural and political context necessary to gain a proper perspective. Most teachers do not understand that race is not a predictor of student failure but rather poor student achievement amongst black students reflects racist policies, that even after slavery, have ensured that black families do not have equal access to resources, quality education, jobs, career opportunities or social programs that have been made to benefit white families. Teachers are often unaware that programs like the New Deal, for example, after the Great Depression, were hardly as inclusive as they should have been—persons of color were discriminated against in public works efforts, home loans, cash assistance, and the programs tended to prioritize the needs of men over women.[6] Heather Hill, Professor in Education at Harvard Graduate School of Education, points out that "once scholars correct for these economic differences among families, including income, the black-white test score gap diminishes in size, and sometimes reverses in direction. For instance, Fryer and Levitt showed in a 2004 study that black students outperform white students on reading at kindergarten entry once only a relatively small set of family background factors are taken into account. In the pre-school years, income—and by extension family economic opportunities—appear to be a driving factor in children's outcomes."[7]

Adjusting Teacher Perspectives

Framing and adjusting teacher perspectives of the so-called "gap" is critically important because if teachers do not understand how racist ideologies manifest themselves in public policy and government, which results in lack of access to resources and opportunities, they are more likely to fall prey to divisive narratives that demonize people of color, immigrants and even women, who are blamed for failure we see in our society. False narratives do quite well in ensuring that teachers either feel inadequate, insecure or worse yet, angry. Bias is complex and rarely should it be understood as solely an individual's problem. I am not suggesting that individual bias does not exist— but rather only looking at the individual to address bias reinforces this notion that the individual is always by default ultimately responsible for what we experience in society, whether it be success or failure, inequality or the achievement gap in schools. This constant emphasis on "individual responsibility" can create real barriers to the type of holistic, integrative thinking we need for teacher agency for equity.

> If teachers do not understand how racist ideologies manifest themselves in public policy and government, which results in lack of access to resources and opportunities, they are more likely to fall prey to divisive narratives that demonize people of color, immigrants and even women, who are blamed for failure we see in our society.

Voices from the Field

I recently had an interesting conversation with Amy Treadwell, who is currently an Assistant Principal in a Chicago public school that serves 99% African-American students, 100% of whom qualify for free lunch. She is supervising a teaching staff that is 81% white with 4 to 5 years teaching experience. Amy is an extremely dedicated African-American in-service teacher educator with 20 years of experience in the field nationally. "All over this country we are talking about the presidential race which has serious implications for race, class, gender and poverty issues, and yet, no one is talking about it at this school," she started. "The janitor told me she was mad ... but that was about it. The kids clearly want to talk about it, but it isn't in the curriculum so we stay on course. To be clear, equity and race are never talked about at school. We focus on curriculum and College and Career Ready Standards. All professional development is about the instructional priorities of the school, which are linked to data and standards. In my professional opinion, the teachers I supervise are not comfortable talking about these topics and they don't have to be. They have been trained not to focus on race, class or any other social or community issues. Where do we see discussions about race, class, social justice or critical pedagogy in the shifts of the Common Core State Standards or EngageNY? Full attention is on effective teaching practices, which is a good thing, but with no room for anything else, it becomes problematic. Teachers believe that school is the one opportunity for their students to move into the middle class and they see this as hard work. They believe there is very little room for error. However, the students at the school come from impoverished backgrounds and the mobility rate hovers near 50%. That means half of the students that were educated at the school last year are gone this year."

Dr. Sana Ansari, an American-Indian teacher educator who wrote a dissertation titled *Deconstructing College-Readiness in an Urban Black Context: Ideology, Discourse, and Practices*, talked to me about the lack of teacher agency and the confusion about what that term really means. "Teachers are definitely feeling less like agents of change nowadays. In my observation this has been going on for close to 10 years. The teachers we call 'good teachers' understand their limits of what they can do, especially about the broader social issues and they learn how to shift their focus. Education used to be a social work movement, about social mobility. Now education is like ... well, teachers are getting the sense that there is a fallacy about education being the great equalizer. While I was working on my dissertation, I had access to teachers working at a charter school in an African American neighborhood. There teachers felt they were making a difference in the lives of those children, but in my observation, their focus wasn't sufficiently on preparing students in academics, which I consider to be vital when we want to make a difference that extends beyond the classroom and school building. Students need the type of skills they will need to get into college, to succeed at college and be competitive in society. The teachers at that school were too focused on soft skills like character, persistence, self-management, advocating for themselves, identity awareness. It was almost entirely character education, which is important, however not at the expense of a challenging academic program. This surfaces a big issue when it comes to agency for equity and what really matters."

Sana, who is currently working in Chicago Public Schools coaching teachers, finds low expectations. "Most of the teachers don't feel like anything they do will have an impact on learning because students are not motivated and they come from families that do not care about education. The tone is usually either paternalistic or overtly racist (i.e., the problem of learning lies with students and their families). In my observation, any skepticism about the teaching profession is more of a deflection of teachers having to actually be reflective about their work. Teachers seem to focus a lot on external factors but not on their own practice. In schools where there are collaboration structures in place, teachers generally tend to feel more empowered and connected to decision-making. However, conversations need to start with considering what kind of learning environment we want for students. This really gets to the heart of the issue—what do we believe our students *deserve*?"

When I asked Sana to comment on what she thinks is the greatest challenge we face in our realization of equity, she responded, "We need to be honest about what is happening here. We need to acknowledge that the real purpose of education these days is *not* about equity; it's to sustain the status quo. Why? Because if we are not talking about funneling resources into schools and at the same time increasing accountability—creating a punitive system—then we are just maintaining the system with some people wealthy and some people poor. If we were really serious about education equity, we would be talking about creating less economic disparity, creating a critical thinking, informed citizenry able to make educated choices in a democratic society and building a real sense of social responsibility. While these ideals might be taught to some extent in some schools, it has to be systemwide. The sad thing is we don't have to totally reimagine a different way of doing things. We have had periods in our history where we had less injustice and economic disparity and more attention on building up the whole society. Injustice is a choice. We need to find a better way to fund schools and educational disparity can't be seen as a poor person's individual problem; rather it should be understood as everyone's problem. Just like segregation, this is a much broader critical problem that must be addressed."

Listening to the voices of practitioners in the field can inject a sense of realism into our discussion about the true nature of teaching and learning and add clarity and credibility to issues that are often clouded by competing interests.[8] It is important to understand that central to the role of an in-service teacher educator is to listen deeply to teachers and to respond to their professional, social and emotional needs. In-service teacher educators and adult professional learning specialists like myself often have access to hundreds of teachers (and administrators) who work in the field each year. Being in the position to listen deeply to educators provides us with critical insights into issues concerning teacher identity and teacher agency as well as perceptions of the context, climate and conditions impacting our practice. When listening to teachers who work in segregated, high-minority, high-poverty schools, we can also gain deep insights into this notion of agency for equity.

Lybroan James, who I mentioned earlier, is an African-American male instructional designer and in-service teacher educator with more than 15 years of teaching experience, five in an all-Jewish independent school, before graduating with a Master's degree in education from Harvard. The first thing Lybroan told me when we started our conversation was how rare it is that he is asked his professional opinion about teaching for equity even though as a black male educator who comes from humble beginnings, you would think his opinion would be a hot commodity. "It's ironic and sad" he says, chuckling. "When I think about this notion of agency for equity, I immediately think back to my days as a teacher in an independent Jewish school where I taught 5 years. As the only African-American teacher, I felt a strong sense of agency in that I knew my students were being exposed to an African-American male in a position of authority probably for the first time in their lives. That was an interesting situation because the Jewish community required new teachers like me who did not come from the community to participate in community events and learn the tenets of Judaism. They expected that we integrate as members of the community beyond the classroom. For them, there was no real teaching and learning that could happen unless each teacher felt fully integrated into the community and deeply understood the culture. Not all Jewish people act religious in the traditional sense of going to temple every week but they were all spiritual in the sense of having faith and/or some belief in God. All of this was an integral part of my acculturation at the school and as a way to be responsive to students. It was through this process of full immersion that I believe we were able to transcend race. Even years after leaving, students have reached out to tell me that I had a huge impact on their lives now that they were out in the world dealing with black folks."

When I asked him to talk about his experience supporting teachers in the field he said, "During my graduate studies at Harvard and now in my current position supporting teachers in the field, I have observed a lot of young, novice teachers who believe they have a sense of agency but I feel it is often misdirected. They tend to focus their attention predominantly on academics to the detriment of teaching the students in a holistic and humane way. Typically it is, I am the teacher and you are the student and I have the power. It is about getting the kids to conform to the dominant culture. I have observed a focus on behavior management rather than developing relationships with children. Understanding social emotional learning, which is popular now, can get us there, but not entirely. Social emotional learning does not directly address issues of equity. Equity is about resources and the distribution of these resources, which if you think about it, is counter American, counter capitalism. Social emotional learning is a good start but it fails to address systemic racism. It seems to me there is always a new term or initiative in education, like SEL, that diverts us from talking about equity. We are becoming more and more segregated and inequality is widening, which is a problem. Now you can measure the performance of a school by the number of white students enrolled. What does that say about our society? Some say segregated schools are the problem. As far as I'm concerned, it's not segregation that matters; it's whether schools are funded and resourced equitably that matters. In a diverse society, there is always one dominant culture trying to invade another culture. As in the Jewish community where I taught, they were segregated and I felt it was just fine. Students left highly educated because they had resources and a strong sense of community and personal agency. This segregated experience translated to agency, self-worth and healing from a history of oppression—which would work perfectly well for the black community. The black community is a fundamentally spiritual people, like all people of color, but we have lost that sense of interconnectedness through slavery, through systematic racism, and schooling that does not address these three elements straight on, agency, self-worth and healing. If that were happening, kids of color would be doing well in school and taking on leadership positions in their community and in society. Unfortunately, teacher educators tend to make a living selling technical fixes to teachers and schools, rather than investing in the adaptive changes we need, adaptive changes that would encourage real agency for equity."

Geoff Baker, a white male with over 15 years as a teacher educator with prior classroom teaching experience in both urban and non-urban school settings, had a lot to add to our conversation. First, he was glad for the opportunity to "get inspired" about an important topic that often gets relegated to the margins, or political correctness. "In general, I've found that teachers' sense of their own empowerment or agency is linked with high self-concept and esteem as well as their compartmentalization of their professional identity as distinct from other identities. I've worked with pre-service and in-service teachers who've expressed complicated internal identities that are lenses through which they view themselves in their professional context; that is, there's more overlap among their identities that can influence, usually, their sense of professional self-esteem. In other words, empowerment seems very contextual. Whether their agency is used to promote equity is another question. I've found that teachers who have demonstrated high degrees of contextual agency seem split on using that agency to promote 'to the greatest need go the greatest resources.' Some teachers use their sense of agency to promote themself within a power structure/ organizational hierarchy; whereas others seem more inclined to promote equity as an altruistic aspiration that further enhances their self-concept and esteem. I've met a few of those teachers, but more of the former."

When I asked Geoff to describe the types of behaviors that he attaches to teacher agents for equity, he responded in this way, "The few agents for equity that I've known seem to have established professional action research habits of mind/practice, and thus can more readily express their agency as an outgrowth of knowing what they're doing, why they're doing it, and what effects it has on others and them self. From my perspective, they seem to be skeptical of their own interpretations of equity and seek others' perspectives and interests before acting. And, they're rightfully skeptical that their actions will directly lead to the intended equitable outcome(s) . . . but they try anyway and attempt to respond appropriately to the feedback from their previous attempts. Some of the more altruistic agents seem to persevere even in professional environments that don't seem conducive to systemic equity. Others seem less resilient; they either move schools or leave the profession. It seems that the conditions necessary for ongoing healthy agency for equity are quite hard to sustain. School communities/cultures are regularly changing due to leaders/leadership, influences on perceived loci of control, and the innumerable other factors that affect personal/social behavior. My gut suggests that teacher agency was negatively influenced by No Child Left Behind (NCLB) and its unintended outcomes such as scripted curricula, compliance-driven leadership and teacher prep that focused more on graduate marketability for example. My early career experiences were influenced by teacher inquiry and action research advocates such as Donald Schön, Chris Agryris, Dixie Goswami and others whose influence seemed to wane in the late 90s. I'm hopeful because there is a trend that suggests we are heading back in that direction. If teachers get psychosocial rewards for their equity efforts, then they're more likely to continue them. Without that, efforts are unlikely given the vagaries of serving in public schools, let alone the complexities of modern, first-world, capitalistic identity."

The good news is that Geoff is not alone noticing a trend that suggests we are heading in a more positive direction. While we are indeed experiencing a time of great uncertainty, there is a notable movement towards re-envisioning what it means to teach and effectively advocate for equity. Teachers and teacher educators are publicly expressing the need to be real, authentic and impassioned about the work, to feel inspired by teaching as a way to effect large-scale social change. This surge of energy for equity is palpable. We saw it in Occupy Wall Street and now with Bernie Sanders, Black Lives Matter, the Dakota Pipeline protests and even the protests against Trump's election to presidency—all of which point to the fact that people (and young people in particular) are pushing us to a future consciousness that demands a respect for diversity, protects the ideals of a real democracy and encourages social responsibility as a natural part of taking care of our collective humanity. What I hear teachers saying is—it is absolutely *not okay* for us to feel confused and disempowered at a time when our decisions really matter in education and that it is absolutely *not okay* for our country to keep such a narrow view of the role of a teacher. We know the power and potential of a conscientiously engaged teacher to transform society!

A New Evolutionary Mindset for the Future

Now more than ever when we are facing extreme levels of inequality, increasing acts of bullying and hate along with mainstream discontent about our current systems' ability to be responsive to the needs of ordinary citizens, we need to harness our collective spirit as educators and model the types of behaviors that will usher in a new future. Imagine what we can do if we can harness the power of 3.5 million public school teachers in our work to build an egalitarian society? There is a growing willingness to engage in discussions about complex issues related to race and class, politics and hegemony and the impact of intersectionality on the teaching profession. We know that our current approach is not working. What we need is protected time and space to do the type of raising consciousness for equity work needed that will lead us to new thinking and new ways of doing. This is not about teachers learning new content or scouring through data—although there is a place for this work in our development. This is more about experimenting with new processes that can refresh our mindset and open the flow of creativity needed to innovate our approach to teaching and learning entirely.

> We know that our current approach is not working. What we need is protected time and space to do the type of raising consciousness for equity work needed that will lead us to new thinking and new ways of doing.

Collective Empowerment

In spite of the wealth of knowledge and research on equity, we really don't have the answers to the dilemma we face. We are right to feel skeptical when an individual or organization professes that they have a solution to the perennial problem of equity in education. However, we do have the knowledge, skills and willingness for Mindful Inquiry to take a look at ourselves, our current conditions of our society, our schools and the policies that shape them. We do have the capacity to embrace our emerging Spirit Consciousness that moves us from the "I" to the bigger "We." What we need now is to nurture and grow our individual and collective sense of empowerment that we can effect change.

Without empowerment, without agency, there is no education for equity. At the very core of teacher agency is this notion that through praxis, we can in fact realize our goals for creating a more egalitarian society. The willingness to engage, to take the time to examine oneself and the role of the teacher within a failing system and consider how we can work differently for equity is a declaration. It says, "Yes, we have gone astray and yes, there is a more humane, more egalitarian way of doing schooling in this country." This is not so easy to proclaim. So many believe that although more than 60 years ago, when the U.S. Supreme Court ruling offered the promise that a child's education would no longer be determined by race, every day across America, for families of color, it remains a promise unfulfilled.[9] Dana Goldstein does a great job outlining how teachers have been embattled by politicians, philanthropists, intellectuals, business leaders, social scientists, activists on both the right and left, parents and even one another for two centuries, and even though we've been arguing about the same questions over and over again, very little consensus has been developed.[10] So, how can we be certain that there is a different reality other than the one we know so well?

We must honor the work of our parents and ancestors before them and look to history and human evolution and remind ourselves that we are progressing. If you think about social justice, civil rights and equity, you have to admit that things are better than they were say, 100 years ago. In 1916, women still did not have the right to vote, for example. We were living with full-fledged Jim Crow. Even when you think of what has happened in history in just the last 50 years, you will begin to realize how much we have evolved. There is a prevailing belief that a crisis, such as the one we face now as a country, can compel us to discover new knowledge, create new institutions and acquire new behaviors. Crisis can be the fuel behind a mass uprising and the momentum behind a social movement. Mental confusion *is* the stimulus for change, and a readiness for a new paradigm. Resolving a crisis enhances our understanding of life, the world in which we live, society and ourselves.[11] Evolution is simply that, the continuing unfolding ability of entities to successfully respond to increasingly complex life conditions. This applies to atoms, cells and human beings and all of their group structures (molecules, organisms and organizations or clans, tribes or nations).[12] And it applies to us teachers and educators globally.

We are all part of the evolution of humanity and in fact, I would argue that being a teacher puts you at the very epicenter of this remarkable transformation.

Where Do We Start?

How do we begin this very important work? How do we transform our skepticism and confusion into a movement that will innovate how we do schooling in America? How do we channel our collective Spirit Consciousness to build a new pathway for equity in education? Let me share a quick, funny story that you might relate to. At a recent professional learning conference I was sitting amongst my colleagues. It was immediately after lunch during two full days of professional learning. The presenter, a tall man with kind eyes, started us off by asking a whopping question, one of those profound academic questions that, in my opinion, are too often posed to educators right after lunch. In response, we looked around hoping that one of us would speak up. After a short pause, one of my colleagues raised her hand. When called upon, she offered up a perfectly suitable answer. Her smart words filled the air on our behalf and we were so grateful. When she was done, the presenter asked her to elaborate. "How does that apply to your work?" It was at that moment that my colleague's eyes widened innocently and cried, "No, you don't understand, that really is all I have to say. All this, these are just words, but you see, I know it's just so much more complicated." At that moment, we all burst out laughing because we easily identified with what she feeling. Eloquent words make the work sound easy when the real, everyday practice is not. What does this really mean and how does it inform our practice?

First, you need to make a choice to embrace a new future, to honor our collective wisdom that tells us *it is time to evolve*. This does not mean we discount past ideas, and the body of knowledge we have built—but rather it acknowledges that, because wisdom itself is an evolving process involving learning and transformation, it must always be about the process of absorbing new and emerging ideas. Wisdom itself moves forward, inevitably; it cannot be grounded in outmoded ideas or beliefs.[13] As such, when we ask ourselves, what does this really mean in regards to our practice, it means we are going to make a choice to engage in new processes that will push us out of our comfort zone so that we are in the refresh mode and can absorb and explore emerging ideas.

The second step is accepting that in order to envision and plan for a new future, you must be willing to tear down false ideologies and false notions of teaching and learning. Most people find that this happens when you take the time to grapple with the hard questions. The hard questions are those that are designed to challenge your unexamined assumptions and reveal your hidden biases and perceptions about your self and the world. Critically examining your beliefs, your convictions, your self and your "teacher identity" within our current context will help you to clear the space so that you can expand your thinking and build anew.

> Critically examining your beliefs, your convictions, your self and your "teacher identity" within our current context will help you to clear the space so that you can expand your thinking and build anew.

Here are three tough questions that you can ask yourself to start. (1) Do you believe that equity is possible in our society? (2) What does equity look like? (3) Does a teacher have the power to move ahead this vision of equity in society? You might want to take a few minutes to reflect on the enormity of these questions now. You will find that the answers to these questions, if taken seriously, cannot be found instantly but actually require some deliberation. I imagine that you will probably continue examining your own thoughts related to these questions throughout the entire time you read this book.

Teacher Voices and Insights

Meanwhile, just like we explored in-service teacher educator voices earlier, I would like to give space to classroom teacher voices as we begin to unpack these three questions. Teachers who work directly with students, families and administrators are in the unique position to offer us more specificity about the teaching experience in the current context, which will lead us to think about the concrete and practical implications of why these questions are charged with meaning. Teachers tend to articulate the type of demands and stressors of the job that may act as barriers to our realization of equity in education as well as barriers to teacher agency.

"If you actually focused on improving the conditions in the schools you won't have the type of teacher turnover you see," one thirty-something year old, white, Jewish teacher from New York told me, matter-of-factly. "Paying teachers more to work in needy schools would also go a long way. The stress and the demands are enormous!" This teacher's statement is not surprising. I had often observed how teachers commiserate around feelings of powerlessness to change the poor working conditions in their schools and feeling undervalued. Poor conditions according to teachers include dilapidated school buildings and kids working in trailers, buildings that look and feel like prisons, overcrowded classrooms, lack of materials and resources, unrealistic schedules that are often created out of compliance, change of leadership, the proliferation of highly paid consultants, broken or outdated technology, no parking, fear in surrounding school communities and excessive testing.

Teachers readily share how school climate dramatically shifts during test-taking cycles. "Are we teaching to pass a test or are we teaching to learn?" the same New York teacher asked. Teachers share how demoralized they feel forcing kids, as early as kindergarten, to sit for hours in front of exams they often don't understand. Leslie Baldacci, author of a heartbreaking memoir that chronicles 2 years of her life teaching in Chicago's inner city writes, "We administered tests on a quarterly basis, tests abandoned by the board years ago. We didn't have instruction manuals because they were out of print. Yet, there was no talk of a more modern or authentic testing method. Just do it, get the results in quarterly and don't make waves was the message. It was just something someone could point to on paper that we did."[14] Baldacci also alluded to what she called "test anxiety" amongst her students. When she receives the Iowa test scores for the students in her classroom she writes, "Five went down in reading, including a girl who had a major breakthrough and experienced reading for pleasure for the first time in her life. Test anxiety?" Later Baldacci later writes that she gave a talk at the office of accountability at the board of education where she spoke out about standardized testing. Baldacci's experience of 12 years ago is still common and even more so with the advent of the Common Core. Even in high-performing schools, teachers share that the pressure to perform on tests is enormous and debilitating and sours a teacher's (and students') sense of agency.

Teachers recognize that working in a segregated school system fuels low expectations and prejudice. Richard Gurspan, a white, Jewish, 20-year veteran teacher leader in Providence, Rhode Island describes this eloquently:

When education is performed by mainly middle-class, Caucasian teachers upon lower-class, minority students (which is the case of my school, where the students are majority Latino and many from first generation immigrant families) there will always be what I am calling "a prejudiced trajectory," the subtlety of which will take many various shapes, the most insidious of which being the dulling of a teacher's natural, social conscience. Teachers rarely advocate for a social justice pedagogy especially in urban schools, even though such an approach would not only be appropriate, but, also, welcomed by the students as necessary and relevant to their desire to be dis-disenfranchised from their society. The reason for this dispiriting lack of cultural responsiveness is because at a fundamental level the minority student is seen as "Other" and in need of being cultured, rather than being seen as an equal partner with the teacher in the mutual process of critical investigation into the platforms upon which a common culture is raised. When this lack of mutual, critical inquiry into the Western narrative is held hostage to the acquisition of knowledge of our dominant mythos, then adolescent thought is suppressed at its root and the minority student finds herself feeling both intellectually stupefied and socially alienated.

If we are being honest, then we should be prepared to admit that the chief, societal function of education has always been, for better or for worse, the acquisition of culture. We, who are the purveyors of education, have been complicit in a systemic indoctrination of our youth into the ethos of the dominant culture, whether patently or covertly, directly or indirectly. This trajectory is engrained to such a degree both into the functioning of our educational system and, also, into the mindset of inner city classroom teachers, so that we rarely recognize the pillars of segregation and prejudice whence it has arisen. Instead, our academic mythology tends to glorify and to eulogize what is "good" in our culture without questioning either the purpose or the process by which we inculcate those morals into our youth.[15]

Even when teachers recognize injustice, they may feel too uncomfortable to address issues of equity head on. Imagine the discomfort a teacher may feel addressing equity (without the proper training and support) when most live outside the community. Communities segregated by race and class put teachers in a very curious position. I have often heard statements like, "I could never live here because it's not safe," "I would never allow my son to attend this school, are you crazy?" or "I can't even find a decent supermarket or a place to get healthy food."

I have seen teachers respond to this dissonance by completely avoiding any topics that might surface this disparity. I have also observed others who do their best to engage in what Singleton describes as "Courageous Conversations," but sadly many end up feeling frustrated because without a whole-school/whole-district approach to critical pedagogy (as evidenced by professional development and funding needed to support the effort), teachers will not experience much success. A few years ago, I visited a public high school in Manhattan where there were no white students and mostly white teachers. The classrooms were bleak and in disarray. I observed a literacy lesson in which students fumbled through what was meant to be a deeply critical and socially relevant discussion and eventually lost interest entirely. It was a mess. The young white teacher, who had prepared some very good discussion prompts, approached me exasperated.

"What do you expect from a segregated school?" she fumed. "You think these kids don't get the message?" I was completely taken aback by her candor and justification.

Not all of what teachers say about teaching in a segregated school system is bad. Quite the contrary. In the study conducted by Irene Liefshitz in which she examined and categorized 17 audio files of New York City public school teacher-to-teacher conversations recorded by the Story Corps National Teacher Project in 2011-12 totaling 16 hours of conversation, including 35 teachers between the ages 22 and 67, Liefshitz found that teachers talk about love, learning, power and purpose. One teacher voice from her study illustrates the type of love and devotion many teachers have for their students and for the joy of teaching. Here the teacher is describing her student:

> From the beginning, she could be very resistant, very confrontational, the type of student where you felt like if you said something to her—even the most neutral comment possible, like "please start your work"—she could snap at you, disrupt the class, walk out of the room, anything along those lines would not be unheard of for her. And on the other hand, there would be these glimpses that I saw in her where I noticed that she had just the biggest heart. She loved listening to other students' stories, she loved empathizing with people, she had the most beautiful smile and when she decided to smile, it would just light up the room. Nothing I am doing is really working, and I am still trying so hard because I believe in her and I want to see this of her more. I believe because I have seen that seed in her.[16]

Another teacher from this same study said:

> As sad as it seems to say this, I don't think the world at large thinks students in the Bronx or students in the so-called inner city are as capable as everyone else. I really don't think the world sees that. I think they write people off, they avoid the entire borough as this kind of wasteland. I think that stereotype is dangerous. Our students are incredibly gifted and smart and they have a lot of potential. They need to be invested in and

publicized and celebrated as much as any student in a thirty thousand dollar private school would be.

In my experience, teachers light up when they share success stories and heart-warming anecdotes about their classrooms and students. These stories typically feature a difficult or challenging student who completely got turned around, or an example of an unexpected academic gain. "I can't believe it, little Johnnie sat still for the entire lesson without hitting anybody!" Many share information about how they were able to build positive relationships with students. Some teachers, who are staunch proponents of the Common Core, share how they work for social justice and equity by not lowering their expectations. I have worked with teachers who make it a priority to provide students with access to "the kind of work students might get if h/she lived in the suburbs." Teachers enjoy taking kids out of the ghetto communities where they live to explore the more cosmopolitan areas of the city and expose them to cultural events. "Some of these kids never leave the few blocks surrounding the schools let alone go to the museum or see a play," one young Asian, New York teacher pointed out in our informal conversation about equity. "I think it's important that teachers do these things and show them what it could be like for them."

These stories are warm and uplifting. Teachers commiserate with each other about the poor conditions of the communities in which they work, but find great joy and reward when they focus on students, the classroom or individual projects. Freire talks about how when we think about exercising agency, we need to understand that there are two types of agency. The first is working for systematic change, that which can only be changed by political power, and the other is educational projects, that which can be carried out with the oppressed.[17] The latter is the type of agency equity teachers are referring to in their storytelling.

When discussing the larger more systemic issues, the tone changes considerably. One young, white Teach For America sixth-grade teacher explained to me, "Look, by sixth grade it's really too late because any real difference a teacher can make can only happen in the very early grades." According to this young teacher, by sixth grade it was already too late. Veteran teachers, I have observed, are more open about their cynicism and resignation that there is a sharp decline in the power of the education system. They share stories of how they are slowly being replaced by new, young teachers who lack institutional history but who are easily swayed into reform initiatives that are not reliable. One teacher I spoke with said, "There is no respect and honor for a veteran teacher any more, as if this profession can be mastered in a 6-week program over the summer. Young teachers may have content but they don't have pedagogy." I have seen how older teachers are often passed over for leadership positions or not informed about career advancement opportunities, especially teachers of color. It is not surprising then that minority teachers, who tend to be concentrated in urban schools serving high-poverty, minority communities, are leaving the profession at high rates. They report it's because of lack of collective voice in educational decisions and a lack of professional autonomy in the classroom.[18]

Teachers Want to Make a Difference but Don't Feel Heard

The Center on Education Policy conducted a national survey of public school K-12 teachers in the winter of 2015-16 in order to further explore teacher perceptions about the profession. Not surprisingly, the majority of teachers indicated that they enter the profession for altruistic reasons. Eighty-two percent of the teachers surveyed said that the most rewarding aspects of teaching involve helping students, by either "making a difference in students' lives" (82%) or "seeing students succeed academically" (69%). On the flip side, almost half (46%) of teachers cited state or district policies that get in the way of teaching as a major challenge, and about one-third cited constantly changing demands placed on teachers and students. Most teachers believe their voices are not often factored into the decision-making process at the district (76%), state (94%), or national (94%) levels even though 53% of teachers say their opinions are considered most of the time at the school level. This is not significantly different than an earlier poll in 2013 conducted by Scholastic and the Gates Foundation, which found that the majority of teachers feel alienated from education policy-making, with only a third reporting that their opinions are valued at the district level, 5% reporting they are valued at the state level, and just 2% reporting they are valued at the national level.[19]

Sixty percent of teachers reported enthusiasm for teaching has lessened; 49% indicated that the stress and disappointments at their school "aren't really worth it"; and 49% indicated that they would leave teaching soon if they could get a higher-paying job. The most notable stressors revealed by the survey are the time devoted to testing, changing demands from outside the classroom, and teachers' perceptions that they lack a voice in major decisions. In the survey sections that invited open comments, teachers wrote in almost equal measures about their desire to help and support students and their frustration with an education system that is too focused on testing.[20]

The findings of this survey mirror my personal observations and my conversations with teachers that reveal several important points. First, the fact that 94% of teachers stated that they believe their voices are not factored into decision-making at the state or national level makes me wonder what kind of difference a teacher thinks he or she can really make in a child's life *that extends beyond the classroom and school setting*. If teachers believe their voices have little or no influence when it comes to critical decisions decided at the state and national levels—decisions that would include budgeting and financial allocations, accountability, human rights and segregation policies, setting priorities around standards, curriculum and assessment, institutionalizing reforms—then teachers are in effect saying that they have no control over important decisions as they relate to the education of students in regards to systemic equities.

Eighty-two percent of the teachers reported that the most rewarding aspects of teaching involve helping students, by either making a difference in students' lives or seeing students succeed academically. What are those things that a teacher refers to that can make a difference in a child's life that are outside of academic success? Forty-nine percent of teachers reported they would leave the profession given an opportunity to earn more money and 49% indicated that the stress and disappointments at their school "aren't really worth it." What are the extenuating conditions that are beginning to weigh so heavily on teachers that their sense of goodwill is diminished substantially? How much do we really value the role of teacher in society and how might salaries further erode a teacher's overall sense of agency? Additionally, there are various interpretations of altruism and there are limits to what teachers are willing to do simply for altruistic reasons. What are the intrinsic rewards in teaching and what are the extrinsic rewards? Both are separate factors to consider as we examine further this notion of teacher agency and working for equity.

There is no easy way to separate this notion of altruism from the type of impact that really matters when it comes to equity. For one, altruism is understood as a benevolent stance that can be exemplified in the caring and loving of all children, especially those who are needy and unfortunate. Enacting altruism in this sense defines the role of teacher as being a provider of a safe space away from strife, teaching academic, social and emotional skills and hoping that these competencies will better prepare children to transcend poverty, the psychological effects of racism (low self-esteem and chronic stress, for example) or traumas inflicted on them as a result of being a part of a damaged and dysfunctional family. Since all of these factors are intolerable and heartbreaking, there is always a lot of work to be done. Teaching in schools that service "at-risk" low-performing, impoverished or racially marginalized students is a humanitarian undertaking. Altruism is individualized and applauded in our society. It emphasizes grit and a growth mindset. We say that with hard work and a good teacher you can change your destiny regardless of zip code or adversity.

In great part due to increasing poverty and persisting "separate but unequal" schools, social justice, democracy, and inclusion programs are increasingly emphasized in teacher education programs worldwide.[21] These programs try to instill a much broader, socio-political vision of education that extends beyond this charitable altruism. Social justice education is seen as a process of conscientization and liberation and as a way to prepare students to critically analyze power structures in society in order to change inequalities through critical pedagogy. My experience listening to teachers concurs with research findings that suggest that these programs and ideologies are quickly undermined when teachers hit the field. Although many teachers work hard to implement their vision of social justice and critical pedagogy within the classroom, many still leave the profession or are considering leaving the classroom because of decreasing autonomy and increasing standardization.[22]

Teachers encounter the stark reality of market-driven curriculum, accountability measures and limits in decision-making in the first year of teaching. This sobering reality hits and there is a critical narrowing that takes place around this notion of a teacher's sphere of influence. With large classroom sizes, complex social issues that impact school climate, paperwork, evaluations and changing expectations with the Common Core curriculum, it's impossible for teachers to do anything else except work tirelessly on the here and now, one child, one day at a time. "I know there is a lot of craziness going on and things that don't make sense, but I need to make tenure so I stay focused on doing what I can do with kids," one teacher pointed out. Teachers are busy putting out fires, staying in compliance and learning new and ever changing "best practices" and programs. "Do you realize how much work is involved in keeping up with changing expectations all the time?" she cried. I nodded, empathetically.

This certainly does not mean investing in children, finding joy in the classroom and being concerned about one's career and job security is not important. It just means that a teacher's life as it is currently designed is a constant struggle with little room for Conscientious Engagement, which implies a commitment to systems thinking.

As a teacher educator who delivers professional development for a living, I can say we have all become expert at ignoring the pink elephants in the room, which are those larger, more systemic issues plaguing education and society. Big social issues are often removed from our most important discussions in education and are relegated to being outside our control, outside "the four corners of a page." It's not to say we don't provide opportunities in adult professional learning for teachers to express their concerns. We design activities and discussions in which teachers can vent, swap horror stories and discuss these "big issues" at the surface and teachers find these moments extremely therapeutic. However, we don't allow the conversation to stay on these topics for too long. They become messy and uncomfortable and seen as moving teachers away from the "real" work at hand. The real work is defined by standards, literacy and mathematics instructional practices. Professional development is not meant to revolutionize teachers. Our job is to focus on immediate, technical fixes, to provide encouragement and support to teachers within the school in which they work. We want teachers to go back into the classroom feeling equipped with tools that will help them improve their day-to-day instruction. We want teachers to be successful at their jobs and we want them to leave feeling a sense of empowerment. Otherwise teachers would never show up to work the next day. Children do depend on teachers showing up, regardless of the circumstances, so this is extremely important work. Helping teachers stay committed to the process, in spite of challenges, is essential. However, how can we make time for teachers to tackle the larger, more systemic issues that would have a long-term impact on schools and communities without feeling like they will jeopardize their jobs in the process? This is the thrust of our evolutionary work! In all my years as an in-service teacher educator, I have never witnessed a teacher who became so inspired by a Professional Development (PD) day or a discussion on change agency that they went back to their school and began disrupting consensus in any significant way. Not that I know of anyway.

Shifting Our Priorities

Teacher agency for equity means we have to prioritize time to inquire into and address the systemic issues that cripple our society and see education as the primary platform through which we can empower key stakeholders to explore innovative solutions needed for large-scale social change, change

Teacher agency for equity means we have to prioritize time to inquire into and address the systemic issues that cripple our society and see education as the primary platform through which we can empower key stakeholders to explore innovative solutions needed for large-scale social change.

that will matter to teachers, children and families beyond the four walls of the classroom. How often do we focus our work solely on things that will have little or no impact on the social, emotional and holistic well-being of the children we service? How many times are we forced into meetings about practices that do not align with what we know to be best for children and yet we do so because we are scared of losing a job, disrupting consensus or worse? And even more difficult is to consider how much of our behavior is conditioned by fear, that we compartmentalize our human identity and our teacher identity as being separate and as the best way to afford a decent life away from the despair and chaos that characterizes many of our most disenfranchised neighborhoods? Are we secretly terrified of the type of poverty and disenfranchisement that we see up close daily and are we relieved that we are removed and protected from the socio-cultural and political realities of the children we teach? How many teachers and school leaders would consider sending their own children to the schools where they work?

Dr. Angela Dye, critical educator, describes the challenge of uncomfortable underlying ideologies when she describes the white peers in her education program at the university. "Like me, they looked at teaching as some form of mission—a ministry of sort. While this mission evoked a level of commitment and passion, it, if not careful, also put us dangerously close to spaces of colonialism. So, unlike me, in that I am a social scientist and aware of the insidious nature of undisclosed imperialism, this ministry-type mission was sometimes poisoned with what appeared to be a hidden need to dominate. When in domination mode, you impose your worldview onto others. When you empower, you respect and celebrate the worldview of others.

When in domination mode, there is one right—one right way of knowing, one right way of thinking, and one right of being. When you empower, you accept that there are multiple ways of knowing, thinking and being—even while acknowledging a single set of standards prescribed by a majority. When in domination mode, a single mindset exists. When you empower, a critical mindset is a must!"[23]

Michael Fullan wrote a great article published in *Educational Leadership* in 1993. It was called, "Why Teachers Must Become Change Agents." This article was written more than 20 years ago and even then Fullan tried to capture the cognitive dissonance. He writes, "Educators today are facing a huge dilemma. On the one hand schools are expected to engage in continuous renewal and change expectations are constantly swirling around them and on the other hand, the way teachers are trained, the way schools are organized, the way the educational hierarchy operates and the way political decision makers treat educators results in a system that is more likely to retain the status quo." To exacerbate the situation, reformers keep convincing teachers that they are doing the right thing, enacting the slogan "Agents of Change" when they teach the Common Core, hold high expectations and demand that children and families perform to standards even though many of them have substandard living conditions, including PTSD, abuses with law enforcement with members of their family snarled in an inequitable criminal system and other impacts of poverty and oppression. Even in the best of cases, children are still experiencing subtle forms of racism and discrimination that shoot down equal access to resources and quality educational experiences. And now, with the growing emphasis on teacher effectiveness and the proliferation of shared leadership models as a way to manage "complex school environments," "teacher as change agent" is linked to databased decision-making. Funders want to know, what is the impact "teacher change agents" have on student achievement? Millions of dollars are being poured into training teachers to be change agents, to transform our schools into highly effective, high-performing places where students experiencing the most egregious life conditions are scoring proficient on state exams and "pulling themselves up" with rigor and grit. Disrupt poverty! Turn high-poverty schools into high-performing schools! The prevailing belief behind teacher as change agent is that the individual, not the system, is ultimately responsible for the failure of students; that it is possible to have a good school with teachers who are regularly transported into an impoverished, marginalized, segregated neighborhood. In this view, school (and teachers) are depicted as an oasis from a child's real life.

With multiple interpretations of terms such as "educational inequality," "social justice" and "change agent" there are just too many different ways of thinking about such ways of working and how they might be developed through teacher education.[24] Furthermore, saying that teachers are change agents if they subscribe to "no nonsense" policies is in fact coopting the true essence of agency as an act of empowerment and critique, not as a way to grease the cogs that keep the machine running. Studies of impact are of course impossible to take seriously with such variation and interpretation. How can we assess and collect data around our work without first having clarity and agreement about the expectations, skills and competencies needed to really improve opportunities for children and families that extend beyond the classroom and school building? We are not even sure what kind of change we are really working for. What does equity in education in a democratic society look like and do we really believe in the possibility of egalitarianism?

One of the greatest perils of our time is the lack of imagination in our practice of education. It appears we continuously perpetuate the status quo, moving the same players from one side of the tennis court to the other and when we scratch below the surface, you may find that similar interests are at play. Where are our independent, progressive thinkers in education and why are we not supporting them in ways that will ignite real change? Teachers have the greatest potential to be thought leaders in our fight for equity, especially women of color who are committed and conscientiously engaged. We need a system that encourages conscientiously engaged teacher leadership and puts imagination at the center of the development of a new teaching workforce.

The Conscientious Engagement Framework

There are several underlying assumptions embedded in the Conscientious Engagement framework that you will be exploring throughout the rest of this book. Some may feel strange and uncomfortable.

◆ Teaching and learning is a holistic practice that involves the mind, body and Spirit Consciousness.
◆ All human beings have a life purpose.
◆ Advocating for love and joy of learning as a fundamental human right is part of the role of a teacher.
◆ Building healthy, safe and nurturing learning environments for adults, children and families is central to our work.
◆ We are at peace when our life's purpose and every day practice are in alignment with the evolution of humanity.
◆ The nature of our thoughts and language, our relationships and how we channel energy are all manifestations of agency.
◆ Exercising imagination is essential for agency for equity.
◆ Your understanding of culture and language influences your ability to teach effectively
◆ Conscientious Engagement is a revolutionary practice with real-world risks.

As you read the chapters ahead, you will begin to slowly unpack these ideas. It is critical that you take on a stance of *reciprocal transformation*.[25,26] Reciprocal transformation is an understanding that everyone involved *must be willing to be changed in meaningful ways*.[27] This means that as you explore the ideas in this book, you should take the time to stop and reflect on one fundamental truth—*you are part of this humanitarian dilemma we find ourselves in*. Once you do that, you can free yourself from the equation and begin to imagine a totally different educational paradigm. It is imagination that is the decisive function of the scholar. It is imagination that serves the ability to expose real, productive questions.[28]

Conscientious Engagement combines elements of Bentz and Shapiro's approach to social work called Mindful Inquiry (MI),[29] which is a synthesis of Critical Theory, Phenomenology, Hermeneutics and Buddhism. This work is also influenced by Social Justice Pedagogy and Pantic's model of teacher agency for Social Justice which includes (1) *sense of purpose* (teachers' beliefs about their role as agents and understanding of social justice), (2) *competence* (teachers' practices addressing the exclusion and underachievement of some students), (3) *autonomy* (teachers' perceptions of environments and context-embedded interactions with others) and (4) *reflexivity* (teachers' capacity to analyze and evaluate their practices and institutional settings). As I have mentioned earlier, this work also builds upon the work of Palmer Parker in that I take into consideration the intellectual, emotional and spiritual pathways in our examination of teacher agency for equity.

Adopting a framework to help you consider and operationalize a new type of teacher agency is a powerful tool. It provides a new language with which to talk about the work and reminds us of our fundamental goal—to work towards and for equity and by doing so, to innovate how we do teaching and learning from the inside out, from the bottom up. This framework helps identify key areas that need our attention as we challenge assumptions, beliefs and practices associated with being a teacher and change agent. It is also a blueprint for professional learning experiences, to engage with individually or with others, and can aid in the design of instructional materials that can help you coach or support teachers who wish to develop agency for equity.

There are three pairs of interlocking principles included in the Conscientious Engagement theory and practice framework (see Figure 5.1). Each pair contains a theory and a corresponding practice.

In the development of Conscientious Engagement, I draw from my knowledge of research in order to provide some level of rigor around the exploration of this framework; however, I do so with great latitude. As a result, I imagine that members of academia may find my approach inadequate. I hope that in this case, academics and scholar practitioners alike will feel

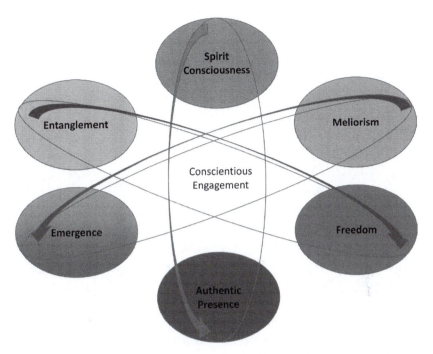

FIGURE 5.1 Diagram of the Conscientious Engagement theory and practice framework.

1. **Spirit Consciousness** (All human beings are made up of mind, body and spirit and therefore have access to a creative divine intelligence)
2. **Authentic Presence** (Integrating one's mind, body and Spirit Consciousness in order to inspire and communicate purpose.)

3. **Entanglement** (We are entangled with some people more than others and these relationships impact how we behave in the world)
4. **Freedom** (Choosing to engage or disengage with people in order to move into alignment with one's authentic self)

5. **Meliorism** (Through human effort we can imagine and build a better world)
6. **Emergence** (Channeling human energy in ways that enable the integration of new ideas for equity)

compelled to refute, add to or further develop upon the ideas presented in this book. Freely expressing one's views as well as welcoming productive critique is in my opinion a democratic stance, one that I value deeply. Many ideas that have influenced my thinking cut across many fields: philosophy, education, metaphysics, theology and social sciences, for example.

Engaging with the ideas presented in this book may feel therapeutic, cathartic and hopeful. This would certainly be a normal response if you identify deeply with the idea that teachers can really be agents for equity. You may even have personally experienced anxiety, uncertainty or social and emotional trauma over the last decade. Perhaps you are one of the many teachers who witnesses injustices and suffering in your school and surrounding community. It's very possible that you are like many who are terrified about the potential impact of Trump, a man who ran a campaign platform of open bigotry, threats against immigrants and Muslims and blatant misogyny.[30] It is important to understand that Conscientious Engagement is not meant to simply be a therapeutic experience. It is a means to a much greater end. Nothing matters unless your thoughts, your inner landscape work, impact the world and especially the children and families in the schools we serve, those who are suffering everyday oppression. My expectation is that by reading these pages, you will consider the everyday implications for your life as a teacher and as a social change agent for equity. In sum, this is designed to be a pedagogical device to revolutionize—from the inside out, from the bottom up. It is a beam of light.

Reflection Questions

1. What has been your primary motivation for entering and staying in the teaching profession? What type of language do you use when you are talking about your work?
2. Who are the change agents in your organization or in your professional life? How would you characterize these individuals? What type of impact do they have?
3. What are the primary barriers to the realization of equity in education and society? How can teachers make a difference that matters? What types of professional learning experiences do educators need that can support authentic teaching and learning for equity?

Notes

1. Ellison, R. (1963). *What These Children Are Like*. Available online at: http://teachingamericanhistory.org/library/document/what-these-children-are-like/ (accessed February 14, 2017).
2. Goldstein, D. (2014). *The Teacher Wars: A History of America's Most Embattled Profession*. New York: Doubleday, p 4.
3. Kumashiro, K. (2008). *The Seduction of Common Sense: How the Right Has Framed the Debate on America's Public Schools*. Teachers College Press, p 75.
4. Casey, L., Di Carlo, M., Bond, B., & Quintero, E. (2015). *The State of Teacher Diversity in American Education*. The Albert Shanker Institute. Available online at: http://www.shankerinstitute.org/resource/teacherdiversity
5. Zimmerman, A. (2016). When is a student gifted or disabled? A new study shows racial bias plays a role in deciding. *Chalkbeat*. Available online at: http://www.chalkbeat.org/posts/ny/2016/10/20/when-is-a-student-gifted-or-disabled-a-new-study-shows-racial-bias-plays-a-role-in-deciding/#.WCDr0hIrKu4
6. Wise, T. (2015). *Under the Affluence: Shaming the Poor, Praising the Rich and Sacrificing the Future of America*. City Lights Books, p. 87.
7. Hill, C. (2016). 50 years ago, one report introduced Americans to the black-white achievement gap. Here's what we've learned since. *Chalkbeat*. Available online at: http://www.chalkbeat.org/posts/us/2016/07/13/50-years-ago-the-coleman-report-revealed-the-black-white-achievement-gap-in-america-heres-what-weve-learned-since/
8. Rentner, D. S., Kober, N., & Frizzell, M., (2016). *Listen to Us: Teacher Views and Voices*. Center on Education Policy (CEP). Available online at: http://www.cep-dc.org/displayDocument.cfm?DocumentID=1456.
9. Williams, J & Whitaker, A (2016). Brown vs. Board of Education is a broken promise. *Time Magazine*, October 7.
10. Goldstein, D. (2014). *The Teacher Wars: A History of America's Most Embattled Profession*. Doubleday, p.5.
11. Natarajan, A. (2014). The conscious individual. *CADMUS*, Vol. 2, No.3., p. 50–54

12. Barrett, R. (2011). Evolutionary Coaching, *Interbeing*, Vol. 5, No. 1, pp. 57–59.
13. Lombardo, T. (2010). Wisdom facing forward: What it means to have heightened future consciousness. *The Futurist*, September-October 2010, p35.
14. Baldacci, L. (2004). *Inside Mrs. B's Classroom*. McGraw Hill, p. 185.
15. Richard Gurspan, personal correspondence.
16. Liefshitz, I. (2015). When Teachers Speak of Teaching, What Do They Say? A Portrait of Teaching from the Story Corps National Teachers Initiative, p. 83. Dissertation, Graduate School of Education Harvard University.
17. Freire, P. (1971). *Pedagogy of the Oppressed*, 30th Anniversary Edition, 2003, Continuum Press, p. 54.
18. Casey, L., Di Carlo, M., Bond, B., & Quintero, E. (2015). *The State of Teacher Diversity in American Education*. The Albert Shanker Institute. Available online at: http://www.shankerinstitute.org/resource/teacherdiversity
19. Goldstein, D (2014). *The Teacher Wars: A History of America's Most Embattled Profession*. Doubleday Press, p. 231.
20. Rentner, D. S., Kober, N., & Frizzell, M., (2016). *Listen to Us: Teacher Views and Voices*. Center on Education Policy (CEP). Available online at: http://www.cep-dc.org/displayDocument.cfm?DocumentID=1456.
21. Agarwal-Rangnath, R., Dover, A., & Henning, N (2016). Reclaiming Agency: Justice-Oriented Social Studies Teachers Respond to Changing Curricular Standards. *Teaching and Teacher Education*, Vol. 59, pp. 457–467.
22. Ibld.
23. Dye, A. (2016). Why we can't talk about racism. Available online at https://medium.com/@ejuc8or/why-we-cant-talk-about-racism-8007efc83561#.fh85rhqf0
24. Pantic, N & Florian, L. (2015). Developing teachers as agents of inclusion and social justice. *Education Inquiry*, Vol. 6, No. 3, pp 333–351.
25. Ravitch, S.M. & Tillman, C. (2010). Collaboration as a site of personal and institutional transformation: Thoughts from inside a cross-national alliance. *Perspectives in Urban Education*, Vol. 8, No. 1, pp. 3–10.

26. Nakkua, M.J. & Ravitch, S.M. (1998). *Matters of Interpretation: Reciprocal Transformation in Therapeutic and Developmental Relationships with Youth*. San Francisco: Jossey-Bass.

27. Ravitch, S.M. & Tillman, C. (2010). Collaboration as a site of personal and institutional transformation: Thoughts from inside a cross-national alliance. *Perspectives in Urban Education*, Vol. 8, No. 1, pp. 3–10.

28. Gadermer, H.-G. (1977). *Philosophical Hermeneutics*. University of California Press.

29. Pantić, N (2015). A model for study of teacher agency for social justice. *Teachers and Teaching: Theory and Practice*, Vol. 21, No. 6, pp. 759–778.

30. Gonzales, J. (2016). Democracy Now!, The war and peace report, November 21. Available online at: https://www.democracynow .org/2016/11/21/jeremy_scahill_mike_pence_has_militant

Six Principles for Teacher Agency for Equity

6

Spirit Consciousness

1. **Spirit Consciousness** (All human beings are made up of mind, body and spirit and therefore have access to a creative divine intelligence)

"Any sound social philosophy must begin by accepting the irremovable fact that human intelligence and all human accomplishments are dependent upon and fall within an infinite, non-human reality."
Daniel Sommer Robinson, 1924

"The invisible classroom—a collection of continuously active neurological and human connections that have an immense effect on learning but little to do with the actual content of the lesson. These undercurrents are always present, sometimes intuited, but rarely perceived and addressed directly."
Kirke Olson, *The Invisible Classroom*

One late afternoon while working at the university, I sat in my small cubicle looking at the computer screen. I had just come out of a very unnerving meeting when I was told I just wasn't working out. The new, white, male professor with a career in education for equity explained that I was simply "too conscientious." These were his exact words. The conversation that ensued was a blur. All I remember thinking was how is it possible for someone to be *too conscientious*?

On the walk back to my small research cubicle, I reviewed every action I had taken, every word I had spoken at meetings, the relationships I had built, the ideas I had brought to the table, the research I had been presenting to the team tirelessly. I was hired as an English Language Learners (ELL) Research Specialist and my job was to gather and share important findings on language learning and bilingual education at a time when bilingual programs were being dismantled. In my research, I found that research and best practices that supported language development were largely absent from the reform programs that were being sold to schools that qualified for federal grant money aimed to improve "low-performing schools" as evidenced on standardized tests. I enthusiastically shared this gap at our meetings and advocated that we develop and disseminate materials that would help schools meet the needs of English Language Learners. How had I done something wrong?

At my cubicle, I sat forlorn. I had to figure out my next move. My husband and I had just bought a small starter house and my son was three. While my mind raced, a small hazy light appeared over the left side of the computer screen. Thinking it was a hair in my eye, I rubbed the lashes several times. The hazy light didn't go away. I leaned forward and rubbed the computer screen thinking it must be something with the screen. I adjusted the nobs on the bottom of the monitor, but nothing. This strange, hazy light just got bigger. When I peered deeply into the light, it appeared to vibrate and the brightness intensified. Amazing! It was like I was watching a vibrating spectrum, similar to a kaleidoscope. The more I relaxed and gazed into the light the more I was able to appreciate its intricacy. It was iridescent and it swirled, glowing from within with these tiny little dotted, multi-colored lights. I turned to the left, turned to the right and it kind of followed me as if an invisible cord came out of my left eye and landed at this one definitive spot. When I closed my eyes, the light was still there and that's when I realized something unusual was happening. Something *amazing* actually.

I leaned back in my chair and surrendered myself to the moment, watching this moving light knowing instinctively that it was ephemeral. I began to feel a vibration as if the feet of a tiny caterpillar ran through my body. This elastic, rubber band seemed to have a current. It was unreal and beautiful. I was suddenly filled with emotion and a presence. It dawned on me that I was not alone. There was a deep sense of love and acceptance for my situation and I knew I would be okay. I knew that I was being challenged but the challenge was an opportunity and an opening for something more, something awaiting me. I unexpectedly fell into the trust, safety and promise of a new day. Several minutes transpired and then I watched as the swirling vibrating light slowly faded away. When it had gone, I looked at the clock. Eight minutes had passed. I thought I'd never see that light again. Little did I know, the light would appear every time a major change in my life was about to happen. I began to call that light my Guardian Angel.

Sharing this strange experience suggests that I am either crazy or that I am deeply convinced that there are aspects of our human experience that are left underexplored but are essential to our understanding of how human beings make sense of the world. Fortunately, over the years, I have learned that there are hundreds of thousands of people all over the world who have had mystical, spiritual or higher consciousness experiences similar to mine; many are actively engaged in studying these sorts of happenings that extend our understanding of our existence beyond the physical world. According to the Pew Research Center, nearly half the American public (49%) says they have had a religious or mystical experience, defined as a "moment of sudden religious insight or awakening."[1]

Understanding Mystical Experiences

In academia, Dr. Douglas Shrader, the late Distinguished Teaching Professor and Chair of Philosophy at SUNY Oneonta, had a mystical experience early in life that changed the course of his scholarship. He wrote, "Suddenly, without warning, my life changed—the world changed—forever. In an unsolicited blinding flash—in a timeless, eternal moment that encompassed creation, annihilation, and everything that falls between the two—I was stripped bare of all my preconceptions: preconceptions about myself, about the world, and about God."

Drawing on classic studies by William James and F.C. Happold, as well as his own personal experience, Shrader began his work to define mystical experiences. He determined that they have the following seven characteristics:[2]

1. **Ineffability** (inability to capture the experience in ordinary language)
2. **Noetic quality** (the notion that mystical experiences reveal an otherwise hidden or inaccessible knowledge)
3. **Transiency** (the simple fact that mystical experiences last for a relatively brief period of time)
4. **Passivity** (the sense that mystical experiences happen to someone; that they are somehow beyond the range of human volition and control)
5. **Unity of Opposites** (a sense of Oneness, Wholeness or Completeness)
6. **Timelessness** (a sense that mystical experiences transcend time)
7. A feeling that one has somehow encountered "**The True Self**" (a sense that mystical experiences reveal the nature of our true, cosmic self, one that is beyond life and death, beyond difference and duality, and beyond ego and selfishness)

If we take a moment to consider these characteristics, it's easy to see how any experience that human beings have that falls into this realm of "spirit" or "consciousness" disrupts all logical, positivistic education discourse. Yet, if we think about our great philosophers, our scientists, and our most inspiring educators, people who have impacted our history, individuals like Gandhi, Martin Luther King, Einstein, Steiner, Montessori—I realize that all of them recognized and embraced this elusive but powerful thing called spirit. Still, I am an educator who has spent years mastering the design and development of lists and rubrics, instructional tools and metrics, finding ways to measure, capture and monitor teaching and learning. I know that if we seriously entertain spirit as a "real" filter that influences cognition and drives human development then we are in fact challenging most if not all of our education practices today. Think about it. What drives our public schools? Observable, measurable, data-based decision-making.

Paradoxically, the notion of teaching as being *soul work* is universal. Parker Palmer writes, "Teaching, like any truly human activity, emerges from one's inwardness for better or worse. As I teach, I project the condition of my soul onto my students, my subject and our way of being together." He argues that to chart the inner landscape of the teacher, three important paths must be taken—intellectual, emotional and spiritual—and none can be ignored."[3] Although in Parker's work, he focuses on the inner landscape of a teacher, if we were to take his approach seriously, we would need to also consider the totality of the inner landscape of every child, every adult, every human being in our school building. If teaching is fundamentally soul work and the great thinkers and leaders of our time, like Gandhi and Martin Luther King, have openly embraced Spirit Consciousness in their work and in the process ignited large-scale social movements, why are we not paying more attention to the role of Spirit Consciousness in education for equity?

Let me take you back to that light that appeared to me while sitting in that small university cubicle. Before its arrival, I was distraught, afraid and confused and yet, as I slowly surrendered to what was happening (which certainly pushed me out of my comfort zone!) something amazing shifted inside me. Suddenly, I was able to alter how I positioned my dilemma in my life in such a way that I could move through it and move forward trusting that *everything would be okay*. My emotions and level of energy changed. I moved from the paralysis of frustration, dread, heaviness and lethargy to clarity, curiosity and anticipation. This Presence had the power to refocus my attention from the negative elements of the situation to what I had learned and the possibility of a new beginning. I knew that I *belonged to something greater than myself* and my fear was transformed into courage and purpose. Although this happened 15 years ago, I still feel the awe and joy of that moment. It has a timeless quality that continues to live in everything I do and even as I write the words to this page, I am inspired and motivated.

It has become increasingly easy to understand after this moment that spirit, and raising our consciousness of spirit, is a pathway and a real source of energy that enables human beings to take on miraculous feats, like working towards the creation of an egalitarian society when so much is stacked against us. I believe that if we are to do this work, we need the courage of individuals to share what they know and help us prepare for the challenge we will face, as well as see clearly the opportunity for teachers to chart a new course in our education history.

> Raising our consciousness of spirit, is a pathway and a real source of energy that enables human beings to take on miraculous feats.

Education Cannot Be Reduced to Science Alone

We know that ontological and epistemological questions are hard to address in education because education has been almost entirely reduced to the world of science and a positivist worldview. Science has become for many the only way to legitimately understand and describe the world. The essential element of the scientific stance is that the universe is purely material in nature, that the universe is relatively uniform, that the universe is essentially available to observation, and that the scientific method will uncover all of the facts about the universe. For this reason, some will always reject perspectives that appear irrational, supernatural or even metaphysical.[4]

However, the field of education, much like the field of psychology, can never have an entirely scientific character. That is because it deals with human development and the construction of knowledge. Human beings everywhere not only grow 206 bones, two kidneys and one heart but they also have a mind with the capacity for images, symbols and concepts. Likewise, according to the all the world's great wisdom traditions, it seems there is this thing called the human spirit that grows intuitions of the Divine.[5] Moreover, every human being, at no matter what stage of their human development, has the available spectrum of consciousness—ego to soul to spirit—at least as temporary states, for the simple reason that all human beings wake, dream and sleep.[6]

Understanding how we learn and construct knowledge is embedded in our understanding of human development and evolution. Civilizations develop and increase in complexity through awareness. Our ability to learn as human beings, to construct new knowledge and apply what we learn, is how we evolve and raise our collective consciousness, to become more adept at living and sustaining life. Learning and constructing knowledge are deeply rooted in, but not limited to, people's culture, which includes one's interpretation and understanding of symbols, language, art,[7] gender and religion. Religion and a patriarchal society, for example, played a key role in how we organized early schools in the early 1800s. Dana Goldstein writes,

> Schools were generally organized by town councils, local churches, urban charitable society, or—in more remote parts of the country—ad hoc groups of neighbors. . . . Two-thirds of American school students attended one-room school houses, where as many as seventy children from age five through sixteen were educated together, usually by one overwhelmed schoolteacher, who was nearly always male. . . . There were rarely any textbooks at hand, and the most frequent assignment was to memorize and recite Bible passages.[8]

As Dana Goldstein further documents in her book, schools evolved in direct relation to our evolving culture, which was greatly shaped by the innovative thinking and doing of courageous individuals who often had to challenge the norms of the day and ignite large social movements. Women in particular, and their fight for rights, became instrumental in transforming the one-room schoolhouse where male teachers dominated and children recited passages from the bible into the type of public schools we have today where the average teacher is female and schools are about learning academics.

Understanding the interrelationship between culture, learning and the construction of knowledge is critically important even now in modern-day society when teachers often fall into the trap of reducing the notion of "culture" to identity politics, when in fact, culture is the total expression of a person's humanity—that which includes ethnicity, country of origin, race, gender and sexual orientation but that which also includes other parts of who we are that are not always apparent and often changing, such as how we express ourselves through language and art, what religion we identify with if at all, how we communicate love, how we understand relationships in society, even how we perceive, interpret and integrate historical events. According to Sonia Nieto, leading scholar on culture, language and education, culture is extremely dynamic, multifaceted, embedded in context, influenced by social, economic, and political factors, socially constructed, learned, and dialectical. Further, she suggests that culture is not a given, but a human creation, dependent on particular geographical, temporal and sociopolitical contexts and therefore vulnerable to issues of power and control.[9] Consequently, as we have seen, culture most certainly includes a person's sense of self as a spiritual or non-spiritual being, whether or not a person connects this spiritual identity (or lack therein) with the notion of religion or God. This is particularly evident when looking at Jewish culture. According to a Pew survey conducted in 2013, 22% of American Jews do not describe themselves as religious, although they are overwhelmingly proud to be Jewish and have an overwhelmingly strong sense of being to the Jewish people. Sixty-two percent of them reported that being Jewish is a matter of ancestry or culture.[10] Conceptually, it may seem possible to separate Jewish culture and ethnicity from religion. However, the unusual and complex nature of Jewish identity makes religion and culture two inseparable strands of a single cord.[11] For example, while observing religious law may not be as important to many American Jews, 60% of U.S. Jews say that a person cannot be Jewish if he or she believe Jesus was the messiah.[12]

Spirit Consciousness and Culture

In sum, culture includes theology, religion and/or any notion of Spirit Consciousness whether the person describes it as a sense of existential awareness, God, or even a life force that shapes the universe. Even when we go back to Rogoff's[13,14] socio-cultural theory that states that learning occurs on three planes, the personal, interpersonal and cultural (the latter includes any and all cultural/societal/communal activities that human beings participate in that are not explicitly designed to instruct but certainly communicate values and purpose), the notion of Spirit Consciousness as part of the cultural plane is evident. Rogoff writes, "Economic, political and religious values tie to such issues as the importance of individual achievement in schooling, the marketplace, and salvation; the appropriateness of competition as motivation to study and to work; and the centrality of literacy as a tool for personal advancement, for the achievement of an informed citizenry, and for knowing the Word of God."[15,16]

According to Dr. Elizabeth Tisdell, one of the leading scholars on culture and spirituality in adult education, there are seven essential assumptions about the nature of spirituality: (1) spirituality and religion are not the same, but for many people they are interrelated; (2) spirituality is an awareness and honoring of wholeness and the interconnectedness of all things through the mystery of what many refer to as the life force, God, higher power, higher self, cosmic energy, Buddha nature, or Great Spirit; (3) spirituality is fundamentally about meaning-making; (4) spirituality is always present (though often unacknowledged) in the learning environment; (5) spiritual development constitutes moving toward greater authenticity or to a more authentic self; (6) spirituality is about how people construct knowledge through largely unconscious and symbolic processes, often made more concrete in art forms such as music, image, symbol and ritual, all of which are manifested culturally; and (7) spiritual experiences most often happen by surprise.[17]

These factors are similar to and build upon Shrader's characteristics of mystical experiences, which I shared earlier.

The importance of Tisdell's work is that she helps us move closer to a more integrated and holistic understanding of spirit as being something that transcends religion and is part of a greater, more universal consciousness. She uses key language such as *awareness* and *honoring of wholeness* and *interconnectedness*. Richard Barrett, the Founder and Chairman of Barrett Values Center and an internationally recognized author, speaker and consultant on leadership, values and culture in business and society defines Consciousness as being *awareness with purpose*. As we pull together what we know from advancements in fields outside of education, we should familiarize ourselves with the wide range of language being used to explore the same phenomena. Some fields of study are likely to avoid the term spirit and instead use the language of Consciousness or Divine Intelligences. Some words appear more adaptable to science, discussions of brain functioning, and cognition, even though it becomes evident that in every field we have all arrived at the same understanding—that there is a metaphysical element of our human experience that impacts how we behave in the world, whether you call it spirit or consciousness.

Social neuroscience, for example, explores the biological foundations of the way humans relate to each other and to themselves and covers diverse topics that include how threatening thoughts and emotions impact the processes in the brain, which directly impacts a person's cognitive functioning.[18] Although I will explore this more later, this means that emotions, feelings and thoughts that once were considered non-measurable (and therefore dismissible in the scientific world) can now be mapped with technology in such a way that we can validate the relationship between thought and the functioning of brain. This has enormous implications for our work.

Spirituality Affects Our Relationships and How We Construct Knowledge

Tisdell has helped us see how spirituality is concerned with authenticity, or the stance one might assume in the world when relating to others. Is this person real and trustworthy? Again, this is about the nature of relationships which should be applied to how we think about the relationships we build in schools with colleagues and in the classroom with students. Finally, Tisdell agrees that spirituality does inform how people construct knowledge and make meaning of the world. In spite of the great work of renowned scientists such as Piaget who did a good job in relegating cognitive development into neat biological stages, an understanding of cognition, which pertains to the construction of knowledge and human development, requires a much broader lens. This is not to say that we have not evolved since Piaget, as we see in the field of developmental psychology with scholars like Robert Kegan who is well known for his work on consciousness as having developmental stages, but we as educators need to be exposed to this type of knowledge that demonstrates learning can come from *an infinite number of human experiences*. Some of these experiences are related to the observable, logical, scientific material world, others relate to the more subjective nature of our interactions with other human beings and, third, there are indeed some experiences that transcend the material plane altogether and include our deep relationship to our Spirit Consciousness, and our sense of belonging to the larger universe, whether you call it God, cosmic energy or a life force—it is a real influence.

Let me share a story that highlights why our work and our language around Spirit Consciousness is tricky. While traveling across the country on a plane for business, I sat next to a young man who after several hours of reading and watching movies began to engage me in conversation. Within a very short span of time, our conversation moved from small talk (his work, his state of residence, an end of a recent relationship) to the topic of meditation. The man confessed that he didn't readily share his interest in meditation with people because it sounds strange, he said, but for some reason he felt comfortable sharing with me. He told me that when he meditated he typically had visions and these visions were having a huge impact on his thinking. Visions? I asked calmly, but I was deeply enthralled in what he had to say. I watched him squirm uncomfortably in his seat as he began to talk about how he wanted to create more time in his life to meditate but he was extremely busy with work demands.

I pushed him gently, wanting him to get to the part I found most fascinating, which was the visions themselves, and finally after wriggling in his seat and combing his hands through his hair, he confessed that describing his visions was not easy. He apologized several times and then explained that he had seen images but the images were somehow combined with deep emotion and there was a sense of knowing and understanding about what the images meant but he couldn't find the words to describe them to me in their entirety. I listened carefully while he stumbled through a vague description and I assured him that I understood. When he was done, I told him visions are like dreams and words can feel clumsy and inadequate to communicate the depth and intensity of the experience. After I said that he looked thoroughly relieved. Our conversation ended by him telling me he would never forget those visions and that he was determined to go back to that state again and again to continue exploring what it all means for his life.

This story demonstrates how limitations in our language can act as a barrier to our construction of new knowledge about the metaphysical world. It also demonstrates how human beings need to receive validation and support from others when trying to express their experiences as they emerge into a higher consciousness. Like this young man on the plane, it is hard to have the confidence when our words don't yet accurately express what we want to say about how this strange visual manifestation of meditation, like our dreams, can impact our thoughts and perception of the "real" world. Without confidence in our language and without being around like-minded individuals, we are more likely to second-guess an extremely powerful and creative process. We might even experience anxiety and suffering as we begin to question our sanity. Have you ever had the experience of trying to share a dream with a friend or relative that impacted you so much that you acted on it the following day? Perhaps you knew it was meaningful and filled with key messages about your life but your words describing it to someone else felt just a little crazy? This is precisely why epistemological and ontological discussions require an understanding of linguistics and hermeneutics, which is the study of language and how we interpret texts and language. Exposing yourself to this knowledge, even just a little bit, can help you build confidence discussing what can otherwise remain an elusive, ineffable topic.

Language Cues into Our Consciousness

Language is how we name, categorize and assign meaning to our world. Language is how we capture and validate our thoughts, feelings and images in such a way that we can become more conscious of ourselves as co-creators of our existence. Language is also how we share our unique worldview with others.

In an increasingly complex world and with mass media pounding out concerted and mostly misguided messages, language has taken on a new layer of complexity and in the field of education in particular. We have seen how language has the potential to manipulate or distract our thinking, especially when it comes to race, class, politics and other constructs pertaining to society. In a deepest personal sense, the positive potentiality of language is that it can become a critical means for the repair of tear(s) of humanity; the structure of language is a wondrous feature of life that is simultaneously stable and infinitely malleable. According to Noam Chomsky, understanding the capacity and nature of language is essential to creating something new, a new organizational structure, a new way of thinking and finding new alternatives.[19] Keeping this in mind, let's look again at the type of language being used when teachers talk about the teaching profession. In the study that I have referenced earlier by Irene Liefshitz out of Harvard University in which she studied teacher voices and surfaced the four essential phenomena in teacher talk (love, learning, power and purpose), she urges educators to seriously consider the following question: What does it mean to think of teaching in terms of *existential well-being*?[20] Her use of the term "existential well-being" relates to "existentialism," which is a philosophical term that refers to how one makes meaning of one's existence, which is directly related to consciousness. According to Hans Georg Gadamer, German philosopher, consciousness is *one's awareness of self as an agent in the world apart from the body.*[21]

Social, cultural and political forces, which have accentuated inequities, have pushed educators to speak out about the dehumanization of schools. Special education teacher Wendy Bradshaw, for example, resigned publicly from Lakeland, Florida's school system in 2014. In her resignation letter she wrote, "I will not subject my child to this disordered system, and I can no longer in good conscience be a part of it myself."[22] Notice the words *good conscience*.

Pauline Hawkins of New Hampshire wrote in her resignation letter in 2014:

> *Ethically, I can no longer work in an educational system that is spiraling downwards while it purports to improve the education of our children. . . . Every year I have seen a decline in student morale; every year I have more and more wounded students sitting in my classroom, more and more students participating in self-harm and bullying. These children are lost and in pain. . . . I know I am not the only teacher feeling this way. Instead of weeding out the "bad" teachers, this evaluation system will continue to frustrate the teachers who are doing everything they can to ensure their students are graduating with the skills necessary to become civic minded individuals. We feel defeated and helpless: if we speak out, we are reprimanded for not being team players; if we do as we are told, we are supporting a broken system.[23]*

Susan Sluyter (2014) wrote, in a letter that was published in the *Washington Post*:

> *I was trying to survive in a community of colleagues who were struggling to do the same: to adapt and survive, to continue to hold onto what we could, and to affirm what we believe to be quality teaching for an early childhood classroom. I began to feel a deep sense of loss of integrity. I felt my spirit, my passion as a teacher, slip away. I felt anger rise inside me. I felt I needed to survive by looking elsewhere and leaving the community I love so dearly. I did not feel I was leaving my job. I felt then and*

feel now that my job left me. It is with deep love and a broken heart that I write this letter.[24]

Arjun Janah, veteran educator in New York City who blogs about the social and emotional impact of education reform writes:

I learned, the hard way, to keep my mouth shut (most of the time) but I never could do the same with my heart. I don't think that this situation—of a closed mouth, but an open heart—is that uncommon among teachers, although I sometimes wonder. Following conscience, one tries to do what seems right, but this can be a very hard path to take, both in regards to the workload that ensues, and from the attitudes of one's "supervisors," many of one's colleagues and, as can happen more frequently than not, from quite a few of one's students. One can work and work and give and give, expecting little in return, except to be left alone to do one's job. But even this is rarely granted, and the psyche can only take so much punishment before it becomes discouraged or rebels.[25]

The widespread dissatisfaction with the current model of education has prompted a cry out from our Spirit Consciousness. It is a signal that we have somehow lost site of the fact that we can no longer narrow our focus on the body and the intellectual mind, but the spirit is essential if we are to be grounded in what is humane, ethical, loving and kind. Not only are educators personally feeling at a loss, but they worry whether the schools we have today are set up to prepare a new generation of citizens who are humane, critical-minded and socially responsible

> The widespread dissatisfaction with the current model of education has prompted a cry out from our Spirit Consciousness. It is a signal that we have somehow lost site of the fact that we can no longer narrow our focus on the body and the intellectual mind, but the spirit is essential if we are to be grounded in what is humane, ethical, loving and kind.

individuals with the skills and knowledge needed to address social unrest, global instability and persisting inequalities. In fact, many would argue that the current education system is hostile to Spirit Consciousness, and perhaps more so for those children who attend high-minority, high-poverty school environments.

Signs of Evolution In the Field

Fortunately, there are hopeful developments in the field of education that have not yet influenced public policy in the Pre-K to 12 arena but are worth mentioning. Recent research, such as that conducted by the Project for the Next Generation of Teachers out of Harvard, suggests that teachers are entering the field because of a humanistic commitment. Attitudes and values such as a sense of mission; solidarity with, and empathy for, students; the courage to challenge mainstream knowledge and conventional wisdom; improvisation; and a passion for social justice are teachers' motivations. The willingness to work long hours, with few rewards, will not satisfy the new generation of teachers. Teacher surveys point over and over again to positive, hopeful, trusting, collegial, caring working conditions as being what teachers most crave.[26] Research suggests that the ability to find joy in everyday life is an increasingly important quality in this time of insecurity and under the pressure of increasing demands for efficiency.[27] In response to this new generation of teacher, education, social work programs and organizations are beginning to innovate our practice.

The Center for Courage and Renewal that was born out of Palmer Parker's work is dedicated to helping educators instill the following core values into schools and the field of education: Integrity, Authenticity, Diversity, Community, Courage, Love, Hope and Renewal. In April 2002 the Association of American Colleges and Universities in the United States held a conference entitled *Spirituality and Learning: Redefining Meaning, Value, and Inclusion in Higher Education*. The conference addressed "the question of the role of spirituality in higher education and proceeded to consider such topics as authenticity that allows for the expression of both heart and meaning, and case studies on transformation of leadership to embody integrity, values, and personal meaning."[28] New York University's Silver School of Social Work has a certificate program called Spirituality and Social Work. In this course, "Students are expected to demonstrate interest and awareness in how spirituality impacts the lives of clients and the values of agency policies and actions."[29] Tisdell, who I mentioned earlier and Chickering et al.[30] study the relationship between spirituality, cultural identity, and social justice, as well as teaching and learning as a spiritually grounded practice.[31] Dr. Elizabeth Tisdell, by the way, is the author of a book called *Exploring Spirituality and Culture in Adult and Higher Education*, in which she expands upon Mezirow's theory of transformational learning by explicitly addressing the spiritual dimension.[32,33,34]

While this work is exciting, we need to advocate for new innovations in our work in the field of public education, supporting and developing teachers and school leaders. The Ross School, for example, located on Long Island with a tuition that runs between $30K and $40K a year, offers a comprehensive, interdisciplinary curriculum system designed to prepare learners to address the challenges and opportunities of an increasingly complex, globally connected future. *The Ross Spiral Curriculum*, written by William Irwin Thompson and designed in collaboration with Ralph Abraham and Howard Gardner, is a literary narrative of the evolution of human consciousness that unfolds chronologically through the grades. The curriculum interweaves knowledge, incorporating skills and content from all of the disciplines.[35] As we stand now, words like evolution of human consciousness do not come up in professional conversations about public school instruction or how we might redesign public schools or create evolutionary teaching and learning environments for children and families who cannot afford to pay $40K a year. Integrative, holistic education that boldly addresses the role of Spirit Consciousness, while present in many private school models, is absent from professional learning spaces that are relevant to the lives of the majority of children in the United States that attend public education. We are seeing mindfulness education and social and emotional learning, but these are still fragmented and poorly directed at managing unruly students, reducing stress and limiting distractive behaviors in the classroom, rather than as a holistic pathway to the humanization of schooling starting with the teacher and infusing into curriculum and instruction. I wonder how we can begin to insert conversations on Spirit Consciousness in the public domain, taking into account the distrust of terms like Spirit that are still associated with faith-based schooling or religion.

Challenges in Framing the Conversation

In Western society, spirituality and religiosity have become attached to bigotry, fanaticism, superstition, fundamentalism, narrow-mindedness and other negative ideas, largely because of many of the bad examples from their practice in history.[36] We see how religious nationalism has fueled intolerance for Muslims in particular, especially following September 11th and in response to the rise of terrorism. Historically, in the United States, as the more overtly Christian influences in the schools were being banned because of the First Amendment, most schools banned identifiable spiritual discourse and practice. In their place, many turned to more spiritual-free approaches, such as values clarification and character education.[37] For fear of violating the rightful separation of church and state, we have limited how educators can help students deal with non-doctrinal inner issues—such as the nature of a "good life" and what is required of us that makes or breaks a democracy.[38] Unfortunately, these limits also prevent us from exploring ways to infuse education with integrative, holistic learning and creating the space to raise a nonreligious Spirit Consciousness about the nature of wisdom, truth and divine intelligence. The recent fervor in national politics that has again politicized religion as a form of national loyalty, a good-versus-evil matrix that hyperbolizes religious fanaticism and terrorism, has made taking a stand for a universal Spirit Consciousness as a unifying force more urgent and simultaneously more complex.

Bernie Sanders's revolution, starting with his decision to educate Americans about what it means to be a Socialist rather than taking the easy way out and disassociating himself from this term, demonstrates the power of challenging the right of politicians to distort the truth by distorting the meaning of words to their benefit. According to bell hooks, "The refusal to name spirit in our work as educators (regardless of your political views) prevents us from bringing our whole selves into the room, which is simply a prerequisite for engaged practice."[39]

Howard Gardner, for example, introduced the learning community to the existence of multiple intelligences.[40] In his research, he identified one of the intelligences as being an innate "sense of knowing." Many experts in the field felt strongly that the better, more accurate term to identify this domain is Spiritual Intelligence because it refers specifically to the evolution and journey of the spirit.[41] However, the notion of spirit as an intelligence and part of our understanding of the learning process goes back much farther. Rudolf Steiner (1861–1925), for example, is the Austrian scholar whose theory of anthroposophy is the basis for Waldorf education. Anthroposophy is a "spiritual science" which trains people to rise above the material and focus on the spiritual world. The purpose of education according to Steiner is "To serve the healthy development of childhood, which means to develop the potential to perceive, through our own self-directed inner activity, not only the physical nature, but also the soul and spirit of each child. Through this ongoing study and research we deepen our appreciation of the spiritual individuality of all human beings, as distinct from but working within and through the sheaths of their given gender, temperament and personality, as well as through the traditions and values of their particular family and cultural community."[42] There are currently more than 150 Waldorf schools in the United States, more than 1,000 schools in the world. Anthroposophists believe that during the first stage, birth to age 7, the spirit inhabiting the body of the child is still adjusting to its surroundings, hence lower grades in Waldorf schools offer minimal academic content. Reading is not introduced until second or third grade.[43]

Maslow made reference to humans having *peak experiences*. A peak experience, according to Maslow, is a tremendous intensification of any of the experiences in which there is loss of self or transcendence of [self]. He defined it as a rapturous emotional experience similar to what religious people might call an ecstatic "mystical experience" where the divisions cease to exist.[44] Peak experiences or "spiritual experiences" according to

Maslow lead to more effective thinking and planning, higher moral reasoning, greater emotional stability and decreased anxiety.

What Can We Learn from the Field of Psychology?

There was a period of time (1800s–early 1900s) where there was an integrated approach to understanding the human psyche. At that time psychologists looked at psychology as the study of the spirit or the soul as it appears in humans.[45] Fechner maintained that the whole universe is spiritual in character and that the phenomenal world of physics is merely the external manifestation of this spiritual reality. His approach to psychology was thus a type of "integral" approach where the goal was to use empirical and scientific measurement not to deny the soul and spirit, but to help elucidate them."[46] This psychology embraced the wisdom of the ages—with perennial philosophy, with the Great Nest of Being, with the Idealist systems, and with the simple facts of consciousness as almost every person knows them: consciousness is real, the inward-observing self is real, the soul is real, however much we might debate the details—a view that attempts to include the truths of body, mind, soul and spirit, not reduce them to material displays, digital bits, empirical processes or objective systems.[47]

The Great Nest of Being is a widely accepted framework for understanding the spirit and consciousness. In its most simplistic sense, it expresses that the Spirit contains the soul, which contains the mind, which contains the body (living matter), which contains nonliving matter, which contains pure energy, which is the ground of being, which is Spirit.[48] In this framework, which goes beyond the scope the book, we can begin to see the connection between Spirit and the mind and more importantly, to understand Spirit as a source of energy.

Energy is the spark, the thrust, the fire behind all purposeful action. It is that which allows us to live fully, to create and to exercise courage and agency. Energy is a currency that is in constant flow, internally and externally between self and the world. Energy is the absolute source of inspiration and the impetus behind any personal or social transformation or social movement. Understanding the realm of Spirit Consciousness as a fundamental source of energy and conduit to infinite and universal knowledge and truth is at the heart of how we develop agency

> Energy is the absolute source of inspiration and the impetus behind any personal or social transformation or social movement.

for equity. Steve McIntosh, author of *Integral Consciousness and the Future of Evolution*, explains all evolutionary systems maintain their order through some type of energy metabolism, thus when it comes to any type of dynamic system, such as the internal or external manifestation of consciousness, understanding the system's metabolism is central to understanding the system as a whole.[49] In other words, thinking about how we nourish and develop Spirit Consciousness is essential to understanding how we can be agents of change and in doing so, amasses the amount of energy needed to act in service with integrity and authenticity. I will discuss more about how we can channel this energy for equity when I discuss the practice of Emergence in Chapter 11.

Advances in Social Neuroscience and Applications to Equity

I want to turn our attention to social neuroscience because advances in this field can help us think about how we might begin to apply the theory of Spirit Consciousness to our everyday practice for equity. Advances in neuroscience are making it easier to study how the dynamics of Consciousness and thought create emotional responses that impact our cognitive abilities. David Rock's brain-based model, that I mentioned earlier, charted out five domains of human social experience: Status, Certainty, Autonomy, Relatedness and Fairness. For teachers, these models can help unpack how specific social experiences impact brain functioning. If you believe a situation is unfair, for example, your threat reflex is triggered and you may no longer have the same cognitive capacity. This has enormous implications for teachers who are in the unique position to design safe and trusting learning environments that enhance student engagement. How might my students' understanding of "fairness" impede or promote their ability to engage effectively with me and others or access new learning? This question has enormous potential. Teachers who are aware can consider the negative impact a national narrative that criminalizes poverty, promotes individual responsibility and alludes to racial inferiority may have on a child's self-esteem or engender mixed feelings about status in the classroom or society. How might a teacher design a teaching and learning environment differently knowing that social experiences affect thought, emotions and by extension our cognitive abilities?

In a society where there is hostility and contempt for the poor (often attached to people of color) these feelings can be easily internalized.[50] Research in neuroscience helps educators heighten their awareness of the potential of their own personal narratives (thoughts) that can impact perception and by extension real decision-making. Research by Princeton's Susan Fiske, for example, found that when hooked up to brain scan imaging machines, and shown pictures of poor people or the homeless, large numbers of subjects reacted the same as if they had been shown pictures of *things* [objects] as opposed to people: a common sign of revulsion and lack of empathy.[51] How might our thoughts or subconscious feelings about poverty, race and immigrant status, for example, translate into overt (or even covert) behaviors in the classroom? We must ask ourselves how we can refresh and protect our internal stream of consciousness when we are constantly bombarded with news of fear, threats to our national security, identity politics, injustice—all of which can hypnotize us into believing that a select group of human beings (the poor, people of color, Muslims) are largely responsible for the ills of society or their own educational failure rather than our need to transform our teaching practice entirely. It really is hard at times to exaggerate how effective the conservative narrative has been in terms of its impact on the national consciousness.[52]

Neuroscience is also providing increasing evidence of brain-based correlates to spiritual, moral and transcendent experiences.[53] Studies such as the one from Harvard University and Sienna University reveal how participants who engaged in a mindfulness meditation aimed at "non-judgmental" thought had a thickening in the right insula and experienced alleviation from symptoms of anxiety and depression.[54] Spirituality is positively associated with long-term survival, lower levels of stress hormones, more optimism, and commitment to helping others in HIV-infected men and women, is another example. General physiological and emotional resilience is associated with spirituality.[55] According to Dr. Andrew Newberg, the Director of Research at the Myrna Brind Center of Integrative Medicine, practices such as meditation lower depression, anxiety and stress. At Thomas Jefferson University in Philadelphia, where he works, researchers have found that meditation can even improve memory and concentration. There is a long history of scientists whose work revolves around making scientific sense of the hidden variables of the universe. John Wheeler, the famous physicist, conducted research that suggests the universe is built like an enormous feedback loop, a loop in which we contribute to the ongoing creation of not just the present and the future, but the past as well. According to John Wheeler, the universe is interactive where the consciousness of the observer actually alters what is observed.[56]

In sum, human beings across all disciplines are embracing this notion of Spirit Consciousness as a fundamental part of our human evolution. It is only expected that we begin to use this knowledge to inform how we prepare and support teachers. Education policy and everyday practice have been painfully slow to centralize the role of Spirit Consciousness in schools, particularly in poor, racially and economically segregated schools where any efforts to do so are trumped by compliance to market-driven, standardized testing mandates and teacher evaluation systems that put math and literacy instruction as the epicenter of all things. Having the courage the courage to surrender oneself to the evolution of Spirit Consciousness, all that moves human beings from an "I" to a "We" mindset and communicates that teaching must activate the mind, body and spirit is the precursor to the realization of an egalitarian society.

to surrender oneself to the evolution of Spirit Consciousness, all that moves human beings from an "I" to a "We" mindset and communicates that teaching must activate the mind, body and spirit is the precursor to the realization of an egalitarian society. It is precisely through Spirit Consciousness that we can tap into the level of energy needed to inspire and lead by bringing our whole selves into the classroom for maximum engagement and transformation. I agree with bell hooks when she says that it is absolutely essential that we build into our teaching vision a place where spirit matters, a place where our spirits can be renewed and our souls restored.

In order for teachers and teacher educators to be agents of change for equity, they need to connect with their Spirit Consciousness, explore it, examine it and learn how it works and what it needs to thrive. Teacher agency is predicated on the understanding of the totality of the human experience and to be acutely aware that we are not alone in this endeavor called life and human evolution. Tapping into a universal network of wisdom of the ages, and knowing that everyone is equal in their access to this universal truth and knowledge is the true source of courage needed to live an authentic life and advocate for authentic living for others. Education is a fundamentally spiritual endeavor. If we continue to conduct ourselves in education without exploring how our inner and collective search for meaning and purpose impacts the teaching and learning paradigm—whether it includes the notion of God or not[57]—we miss what is most essential to our human experience.

Reflection Questions

1. Have you had a spiritual, mystical or dream experience that permanently changed how you view the world? What do we mean when we say "trust your intuition"? Is having courage something you can teach and develop?
2. How might a person's spiritual outlook impact how he makes sense of new knowledge and makes meaning?
3. How do fear and other threatening emotions affect cognition? How does the media influence what you

think and feel about specific groups in society? What can you do to mitigate these negative influences on our thinking?

4. What would change in your approach to teaching if you considered Spirit Consciousness as a "filter" through which all human beings receive and process information?

Notes

1. Pew Forum on Religion & Public Life (2009). *Eastern, New Age Beliefs Widespread. Many Americans Mix Multiple Faiths.* Pew Research Center. Available online at: http://www.pewforum.org/files/2009/12/multiplefaiths.pdf

2. Shrader, D. (2008). Seven characteristics of mystical experiences. *Proceedings of the 6th Annual Hawaii International Conference on Arts and Humanities.* Honolulu, HI.

3. Palmer, P. (1998). *The Courage to Teach: The Inner Landscape of a Teacher's Life.* John Wiley & Sons.

4. Newberg, A. (2014). *The Metaphysical Mind: Probing the Biology of Philosophical Thought.* CreateSpace Publishing.

5. Wilbur, K. (2011). *Integral Psychology. Consciousness, Spirit, Psychology, Therapy.* Shambhala.

6. Ibid.

7. Tisdell, E.J. (2003). *Exploring Spirituality and Culture in Adult and Higher Education.* San Francisco: Jossey-Bass.

8. Goldstein, D. (2014). *Teacher Wars: A History of America's Most Embattled Profession.* Doubleday Press.

9. Nieto, S. (2008). Culture and education. In *Yearbook for the National Society for the Study of Education.* Blackwell Publishing, pp. 127–142.

10. Pew Forum on Religion & Public Life (2013). *A portrait of Jewish Americans.* Pew Research Center. Available online at: http://www.pewforum.org/2013/10/01/jewish-american-beliefs-attitudes-culture-survey/

11. Morris, L. A. (2013). Religion matters: Beware of the American cultural Jew. Haaretz.com, October 9. Available online at: http://www.haaretz.com/opinion/.premium-1.551291

12. Pew Forum on Religion & Public Life (2013). *A portrait of Jewish Americans*. Pew Research Center. Available online at: http://www.pewforum.org/2013/10/01/jewish-american-beliefs-attitudes-culture-survey/

13. Rogoff, B. (1990). *Apprenticeship in Thinking: Cognitive Development in Social Context*. New York: Oxford University Press.

14. Rogoff, B. (1995). Observing sociocultural activity on three planes: participatory appropriation, guided participation, and apprenticeship. In J.V. Wertsch, P del Rio., & A. Alvarez (Eds.), *Sociocultural Studies of Mind*. New York, NY: Cambridge University Press, pp. 139–164.

15. Rogoff, B. (1990). *Apprenticeship in Thinking: Cognitive Development in Social Context*. New York: Oxford University Press.

16. Rogoff, B. (1995). Observing sociocultural activity on three planes: participatory appropriation, guided participation, and apprenticeship. In J.V. Wertsch, P del Rio., & A. Alvarez (Eds.), *Sociocultural Studies of Mind*. New York, NY: Cambridge University Press, pp. 139–164.

17. Tisdell, E. (2003) *Exploring Spirituality and Culture in Adult and Higher Education*. San Francisco: Jossey-Bass, p. 28.

18. Rock, D. (2008). SCARF: A brain-based model for collaborating and influencing others. *Neuroleadership Journal*. No. 1.

19. Raskin, M. (2014). *Masters of Mankind Essays and Lectures, 1969–2103*. Noam Chomsky, Foreword. Chicago: Haymarket Books.

20. Liefshitz, I. (2015). When Teachers Speak of Teaching, What Do They Say? A Portrait of Teaching from the Voices of StoryCorps National Teachers Initiative. Doctoral Dissertation, Harvard Graduate School of Education.

21. Gadamer, H. (1976). *Philosophical Hermeneutics*. University of California Press

22. Wilkins, V. (2014). Special education teacher with doctorate degree quits with powerful resignation. ABC News. Available online at: http://abcnews.go.com/Lifestyle/special-education-teacher-doctorate-degree-quits-powerful-resignation/story?id=34973579

23. Hawkins, P. (2014). My resignation letter. April 7. Available online at: http://paulinehawkins.com/2014/04/07/my-resignation-letter/

24. Adwar, C. (2014). This teachers alarming newsletter shows how much schools have changed since you were a kid. *Business Insider*. Available online at: http://www.businessinsider.com/susan-sluyters-resignation-letter-sums-up-common-core-concerns-2014-4

25. Janah, A. (2014). Thanksgiving thoughts—On turkeys, teachers, soldiers and conscience. The Humble Subject Teacher blog. http://subject-teacher.blogspot.com/2014_11_01_archive.html

26. Simon, N. & Johnson, S. (2015). *Teacher Turnover in High-Poverty Schools: What We Know and Can Do*. Project on the Teachers for the Next Generation. Harvard School of Education.

27. Määttä, K & Uusiautti, S. (2012). Pedagogical authority and pedagogical love-Connected or incompatible? *International Journal of Whole Schooling*, Vol. 8, No. 1, p. 21.

28. Groen, J. (2009). Moving in from the fringes of the academy: Spirituality as an emerging focus in the Canadian professional faculties of business, education, and social work. *The Journal of Educational Thought*, Vol. 43, No. 3, pp. 223–244.

29. NYU Silver School of Social Work. Spirituality and Social Work Program Overview. Available online at: http://socialwork.nyu.edu/alumni/continuing-education/post-masters/spirituality.html

30. Chickering, D. Dalton, J. & Stamm, L. (2006). *Encouraging Authenticity & Spirituality in Higher Education*. San Francisco, CA: Jossey Bass.

31. As cited in Groen, J. (2009). Moving in from the fringes of the academy: Spirituality as an emerging focus in the Canadian professional faculties of business, education, and social work. *The Journal of Educational Thought*, Vol. 43, No. 3, pp. 223–244.

32. Mezirow, J. (1985). Concept and action in adult education. *Adult Education Quarterly*, Vol. 35, No. 3, pp. 142–152.

33. Mezirow, J. (1995). Transformation theory of adult learning. In M. Welton (Ed.), *In Defense of the Lifeworld: Critical Perspectives on Adult Learning*. pp. 39–70.

34. Tisdell, E.J. (2003) *Exploring Spirituality and Culture in Adult and Higher Education*. San Francisco: Jossey-Bass.

35. Ross Institute and Ross Learning System: http://rossinstitute.org/

36. Clarken, R. H. (2009). Paper presented at the American Educational Research Association Annual Meeting, San Diego, April 12–17, 2009.

37. Ibid.

38. Palmer, P.D. (2011). *Healing the Heart of Democracy*. San Francisco: Jossey-Bass, p. 123.

39. hooks, b (2003). *Teaching Community: A Pedagogy of Hope*. Routledge.

40. Gardner, H. (1999). *Intelligence Reframed: Multiple Intelligence for the 21st Century*. New York: Penguin Putman.

41. Rios, R. & Talwar, S. (2009). *Transcensory education: expanding our understanding of intelligence.* Real World Dialogue Blog. Available online at: https://realworlddialogue.com/2009/10/28/transcensory-education-expanding-our-understanding-of-intelligence/

42. The International Association for Steiner/Waldorf Early Education. Availalbleonlineat:http://www.iaswece.org/Files/Mandate_Groups/The_Universal_spirit_EN.pdf

43. Boston, R. (1996). Anthroposophy: Rudolf Steiner's 'spiritual science.' Available online at: http://www.waldorfcritics.org/articles/Anthroposophy_AU.html

44. Maslow, A.H. (1987). *Motivation and Personality (3rd ed.).* New York, NY: Harper & Row. pp. 138, 165.

45. Wilbur, K. (2011). *Integral Psychology. Consciousness, Spirit, Psychology, Therapy.* Shambhala.

46. Ibid. (142/6559)

47. Ibid.

48. Wilber, K. (1995). *Sex, Ecology, Spirituality.* Boston, MA: Shambhala Publications, Inc.

49. McIntosh, S. (2007). *Integral Consciousness and the Future of Evolution.* Paragon House, p. 26.

50. Wise, T. (2015). *Under the Affluence: Shaming the Poor, Praising the Rich, and Sacrificing the Future of America.* City Lights Open Media p. 103.

51. Ibid.

52. Ibid., p. 93

53. Beauregard, M. & O'Leary, D. (2007). *Spiritual Brain.* New York: HarperOne.

54. Santarnecchi, E., D'Arista, S., Egiziano, E, Gardi, C, Petrosino, R, et al. (2014). Interaction between Neuroanatomical and Psychological Changes after Mindfulness-Based Training. *PLoS ONE*, Vol. 9, No. 10, e108359. doi:10.1371/journal.pone.0108359

55. Ironson, G. (2002). The Ironson-Woods Spirituality/Religiousness Index Is Associated with Long Survival, Health Behaviors, Less Stress and Low Cortisol in People with AIDS. *Annals of Behavioral Medicine.* Vol. 24, No. 1, pp. 34–48.

56. Harvey, A. (2009). *The Hope: A Guide to Sacred Activism.* Hay House Press.

57. Palmer, P. (2011). *Healing the Heart of Democracy*, San Francisco: Jossey-Bass, pp. 123–124.

7

Authentic Presence

2. **Authentic Presence** (Integrating one's mind, body and Spirit Consciousness in order to inspire and communicate purpose)

Verse 49
The Sage has no fixed heart of his own
Those who look at him
*   see their own hearts*
Those who are good he treats with goodness
Those who are bad he also treats with goodness
*   because the nature of his being is good*
Those who are truthful he treats with truth
Those who are not truthful he also treats with truth
*   because the nature of his being is truthful*
The Sage lives in harmony with all below Heaven
He sees everything as his own self
He loves everyone as his own child
All people are drawn to him
*   Every eye and ear is turned toward him*
Lao Tzu, Tao Te Ching

When I walk into a room full of educators there is always a moment of pause when I ask myself, why am I here? What is the most important thing? How can I communicate a sense of urgency as well as a deep sense of compassion for the everyday practice of teaching and learning? Opening myself up to draw from the wisdom of my mind, body and Spirit Consciousness in the quiet moments that lead up to my work is the gateway to Authentic Presence.

Perhaps you have heard of the Sanskrit word Namaste? It means there is a divine spark inside of each of us that is located in the heart chakra. I start our discussion of the practice of Authentic Presence by referring to Namaste because unlike the words we have in English, Namaste seems to get closer to capturing the essence of Authentic Presence. There are many meanings or translations of this Hindu word that is often used as a greeting between two people. One meaning is, "I honor the sacredness and equality in us all." Another is, "I honor the place in you, which is love, truth, light and peace."[1]

In the practice of Authentic Presence, I bring two English words together, Authenticity and Presence, to describe how we must bring one's whole self (mind, body and Spirit Consciousness) into the craft of teaching and learning in order to communicate purpose and inspire. It is only through the full integration of the mind, body and Spirit Consciousness that we are released from the constraining duality of mind and body and are infused with the level of energy needed to inspire and communicate purpose. Authentic Presence is a deep communion with our creative self and the divine intelligence of others. As you begin to consider and engage in the practice of Authentic Presence, you will be amazed at how you can manifest your purpose in ways that are good for all involved. Understanding the totality of Authentic Presence as a way of being and interacting with oneself and the world, rather than a single ritual or meditation, is critical. Spirit comes from the word "spiritus," which means "breath." In this regard, spirit, like our daily breath, is an integral part of the human essence. It sustains the individual throughout life and beyond.[2] Looking at it in this way, Authentic Presence has the power to transform the teaching and learning dynamic into meaningful soulful interactions in which the teacher and the student experience joy and the awe of every day discoveries.

I started formalizing my thoughts around this notion of Authentic Presence when I went back to teaching children. I had been working with adults, supporting and coaching teachers and leaders for more than a decade, but the practice of Authentic Presence as a method began to take shape in my (re)union with children. I understand now that this is because children in their natural state are authentic and present. They are vulnerable and receptive. Going back into the classroom at this critical point in my career in many respects was perfectly designed for me to test my theory of Conscientious Engagement and consider what we can learn from children about the nature of authenticity and agency in a school environment.

Authentic Presence in the Real World

The challenge became how to concretize my theory into everyday practices. I needed a method and a language to describe the internal and external processes involved in reaching this state that I was hopeful could be developed by others. As I explained earlier in this book, Conscientious Engagement must be understood as both a theory and a practice, so the essential question remains—how do we develop practice without experiencing? I also knew that Authentic Presence as a practice would most likely be different in some respects when working with children as compared to adults. I will address my thinking as it pertains to both.

The Common Core was well underway. Three teachers had quit the 6th grade class by November. It was a brand new charter school that wanted to provide high-risk, high-needs students with a technology-rich education. The school was predicated on free laptops, organic lunches and relationship-building. Part of the teachers' job was to serve lunch to the students in the classroom in order to build community and ensure that the students ate healthy food. The lunch was contracted in from another borough and often arrived late. The school was staffed with novice teachers; most had less than three years' experience. The question, "Why don't they come to school with a pencil?" rang through the halls almost every day. It was this recurrent question that communicated to me everything wrong with our failure to realize education for equity.

It was shocking to me how the Board and new leadership considered opening a new charter school to serve predominantly poor, high-needs students and staffing it with young novice teachers with less than three years' experience to be less than criminal. The needs of the children were so complex that even for someone like me, teaching effectively and with dignity was an enormous undertaking. In just the first week, I sat down to cry.

Remember, by that time in my career, the theory of Conscientious Engagement had already started developing in my mind and in my writing. So, when I took on this challenge, I made a promise to myself that I would practice applying my big ideas. Much of what I did was an experiment, but the experiment was not in a vacuum. My behaviors and choices in the classroom were based on teaching experience, years of reading and research and imagining. The first thing I committed to doing was to start every day meditating on questions such as: Why am I here? What is the most important thing? How can I communicate a sense of purpose as well as a deep sense of compassion? How can I inspire? Like I said, in this position I was charged with teaching sixth graders the new Common Core standards, which were at that time still new; we did not have access to many of the resources we have today, such as what you might find on EngageNY (a website designed to support educators on the implementation of the standards). I had to design and develop my own curriculum, find materials (my class had no books and it was January when I started), gather resources, buy supplies, build relationships with my students as well as with my young colleagues, set classroom structures, integrate behavior management and develop life skills routines. Since many teachers had abandoned the job, the children were angry or apathetic, making my practice of Conscientious Engagement that much more important.

I woke up early in the morning. I would sit at my desk, ask myself the three questions and allow the questions to sit inside me while I took the time to breathe in the quiet moments of the morning. This did not take very long but sometimes (especially at first) it was hard not to focus on the list of other things that I knew I could be doing. I did this routine with a hot cup of coffee. Some people think that meditation can only look one way but in the life of a busy educator, meditation happens in many different ways, and has a wide range of durations and purposes. For me, the point of meditation is *you* establish the routine that feels natural and comfortable for you, as long as it is a time in which you surrender yourself to a moment of silence in which you ruminate on important questions without putting pressure on yourself to answer or solve them. Shortly after I reflected on these questions, I would turn on the computer and start searching for a meaningful quote that I would present to my students that same morning. The quote would be aligned to my literacy theme of the unit and taken from an author, world figure, community leader or famous personality. I made a point to prioritize quotes from smart and dynamic people that reflected the diversity of my students. This was not always easy. During this process, I sadly found that there is a dearth of information about the contributions of Latinos, for example. Afterwards, I'd create a smart board page that was visually enticing that highlighted both the quote and the author followed by one to two open-ended questions to ponder.

Once at the school, I would get ready for morning meeting by making sure the classroom was neat and welcoming. Kids strolled in at varying times and many who lived far away would arrive late, but they all would be greeted by my Authentic Presence and the quote on the smart board page. Often the children would read it on their own and make side comments as they unpacked their things but they all knew that we would take the time to discuss it together. On the first day of the ritual, I was very clear about the process and the purpose of setting the stage for the day. It was easy to do, frankly; they were hungry for someone who had for many years learned how to nurture the goodness in self and in others that emanated a calm, safe space and a meaningful routine they could expect daily.

I'd first read the quote aloud several times and then ask a volunteer or two to read it. We would follow with a brief discussion of the importance of the public figure. The kids enjoyed seeing the picture of the face or the cover of a book. Next, we'd explore the meaning of the quote by relating it to our own lives. The meeting would end with me reading the questions that would get the students thinking deeper about the topic throughout the day. I would always say, *"There are no right or wrong answers to these questions, they are just here to get you thinking. Keep them in mind as you engage with others and learning activities throughout the day. Tomorrow I will ask you to share your thoughts with the class."* This daily meditation-like practice that would set the stage for the rest of the day and link to the next day, that started with my own inner work at home, had such a profound impact on the climate and culture in my classroom that within a few weeks, teachers in the school were coming in to my room to ask, what is it that you are doing? I was beginning to understand the power of Authentic Presence.

***

"What does it mean when an author describes a person as **bright***?"*

Several hands shoot up. A tall, olive complexioned girl with hair rippling down her back calls out, "It means you're smart!"

"Good!" I say and turn to my smart board. I draw a smart cartoon character with a thought bubble hovering over his head. Inside the bubble, I draw a light bulb with five sparks sprouting out from all sides.

"Have you guys ever seen this?" Most nod and a few snicker. I add a mustache and glasses in quick animation style. "Calling someone *bright* means their ideas are like light bulbs that go off in their brains," I explain smiling. "Smart is a trait that belongs to those who have ideas that bring light to darkness."

Pause. Breath in and out. Wait. There is silence.

I look around. I am acutely aware that I still have one hundred percent attention; each day their attention span expands. My heartbeat quickens. One boy with big brown eyes and a sharp needled Mohawk is at the edge of his seat. "Light to darkness?" he repeats aloud, still trying to figure it out. Several eyes move towards him and wait to see if he has more to say. There is a giggle in the back, and it is delightful so I smile.

I have a young, white resident TFA teacher in the room. She is watching me and the room carefully. It's been two months of intensive morning meetings and they're really making a difference. The students' ability to listen to each other is developing.

I write the word

ENLIGHTENMENT

I tap the ink pen icon on my menu panel so that I can write **LIGHT** in ENLIGHTENMENT in red.

"Has anyone ever heard of this word, enlightenment?"

The kids shake their heads. A couple laugh nervously.

"Enlightenment is what all the great thinkers and sages aim to achieve," I tell them. "It's a state of grace in which there's perfect harmony between your mind and spirit—between what you learn in school and the journey of your soul."

I can't believe what I'm saying but the words flow out as if someone else is talking through my mouth and lips. The resident teacher looks at me, bewildered. This way of speaking to the children is new. I hold my pause. In the pause, I look at their eyes. They are so wide. I wonder for a split second if I have said too much for a sixth grader. I decide to move ahead and trust their ability to grasp what I'm saying.

"Many believe that true 'smarts' comes from knowledge, yes!" I exclaim, "but also, it comes from the courage of a person's spirit to use the information, to use the knowledge wisely and ethically."

I get a few blank stares at this point, but they are still riveted so I keep nodding my head like a spring and smiling as if they are all with me making sense of every word. A few murmurs bubble up which tells me I have to say something to pull it together quick. My heart is beating fast. How do I communicate to them that it's perfectly okay even if they don't understand *every word* I'm saying, that if they allow the moment to exist, in that space, the words together and the feeling in the room will make perfect sense?

I repeat, "Enlightenment is the courage of a person's spirit to use knowledge wisely and ethically."

Pause. Breathe in and out. Wait.

"You mean, just like Dr. Martin Luther King wrote in his essay?" It was the voice of the sassiest girl in the class and I am stunned. We had been struggling for several days on Martin Luther King's essay called "The Purpose of Education," which is rich in academic vocabulary and a complex read for sixth grade.

"Yeeees!!" I scream. The kids begin to nod now and there is murmuring and excitement. "Remember what Dr. King said about education being not just knowledge but about character? Let me say it one more time and if you want to write it down on your paper—that would be fine too. Enlightenment is the courage of a person's spirit to use knowledge wisely and ethically."

A few kids scribble the words down. I look over at my resident teacher who is shaking her head in disbelief and grinning.

"So, now, let's talk some more about how writers use metaphors to communicate," I say. "For example, why might a writer use the word ogre to describe a person?"

The class bursts out laughing. "It means he's probably really mean and ugly!" The spell of ENLIGHTENMENT is broken and we all laugh from relief.

***

Authenticity as Presence

Lloyd Kornelsen describes authenticity in education as being directly related to presence. He suggests it is what we find after we transition from *a way of doing* to *a way of being*. According to Kornelsen, this notion corresponds to Dunne's description of the two forms of Aristotelian knowledge, *techne* and *phronesis*.[3] Techne is knowledge that is possessed by the individual after having studied and practiced, like a craft. Phronesis, on the other hand, is knowledge that comes from wisdom, which is one's awareness of self, one's understanding of the world and all the complex relationships within it and the ability to accept and account for universal truths. This second knowledge elevates the craft so that all who are involved in the experience are fully realized through ultimate engagement. Dunne argues that teaching (or any form of human interaction) cannot be reduced to technique because teaching is not a process of making objects but a practice of engaging in human interactions.[4]

The idea of authenticity[5] places emphasis on the qualities of an educator as a person, on the nature of self. It expresses a need for the genuine self within a community, consistency between values and actions, relationships with others, and maintaining a critical perspective.[6] To be able to express the genuine self, Cranton and Carusetta suggest, people need to know who the self is.[7] How do we get to know who we really are? One way to do this is to become aware of the nature of your thoughts, which at first dominate your inner world. These thoughts are often tapes that we adopt from our parents, the society or from all of the distractions we experience on a day-to-day basis. The process of knowing who you are is becoming aware of the thoughts that dominate your mind and removing them one by one so that you can slip into the realm of silence and pure breath—which is the essence of your Spirit Consciousness, and your inspiration. This heightening of awareness of thought can feel scary or uncomfortable at first because we all have thoughts that are filled with guilt, shame and other hateful things that may not represent the ideal vision of ourselves. But it is precisely in this moment that we become aware that there is a Consciousness separate from thought, and Consciousness has the power to look upon thought with love, compassion and forgiveness, all of which frees ourselves from thought completely. This great "letting go" of our attachment to thought (that which binds us to the material worldview) is what we call meditation and surrender.

Vulnerability in the Classroom

Authentic Presence, or the great "letting go" as a practice, is not easy and is even more difficult in the context of the contemporary public school classroom. I have found that many teachers are afraid of "letting go" of themselves, which results in feeling vulnerable in front of students. Vulnerability is a byproduct of bringing one's whole self, or Spirit Consciousness, into teaching, because all human beings can be viewed as flawed or imperfect in some way. That is part of being human. Furthermore, we have been socialized to attach elements of our identity and the role of a teacher to power, authority and other manifestations of ego. Power manifests in our behavior through language, relationships, choices in curriculum and instruction, classroom management, how we assess and evaluate students etc.—all of this results in a breakdown of Authentic Presence. Authentic Presence is the surrender of power and ego and our need to always be in control. I am not suggesting that teachers should have chaotic, disorganized, unstructured classrooms. To relinquish control in the context of our discussion of Authentic Presence means that we "let go" of our assumptions (thoughts) about how knowledge is constructed and what truth is (that which is related to meaning making). The teacher who exercises Authentic Presence is both a teacher and student simultaneously, because they come into the situation with cleared space; only through interactions with others does the space reshape and reform itself. As teacher, he/she is charged with designing lessons rich with debate, open-ended questions, riddles and problems for solving but in the very letting go to the open nature of the construction of knowledge and meaning-making, the teacher now becomes receiver and observer of students who will demonstrate their own construction of knowledge and the truths they encounter along the way.

Understanding how manifestations of power, ego and our need to be in control can break down authentic learning takes time because we are often unaware of our thoughts and have not gone through the work of clearing the inner space; therefore, thoughts determine how we behave rather than Consciousness. What is the nature of our thoughts?

We are living at a time when we are bombarded with thoughts generated by market-driven expectations, racial tensions and economic insecurity. Economic insecurity fuels thoughts that drive us harder to meet expectations that fuel thoughts that are related to racial tensions and the need for "them" to speak the English language, for example, or pass a test. All of these thoughts that inhabit our being become one big, muddled justification for why *we must stay in control*. The media exacerbates the situation as our thoughts are now influenced by leaders that tell us we need to exert more power, more control, and more authority—over certain groups in particular. So, imagine how these thoughts may impact our work for Authentic Presence. It may feel like you are drowning in thought. It is so easy to get frantic, panic and paddle your arms wildly thinking that force and strength will save you. Yet, any good lifeguard will tell you that you must relax and remove yourself from panic and fear and learn to embrace the properties of water to float and rise above. The more a teacher refuses to remove his or herself from the distractions and practice the everyday surrender of thoughts related to power, privilege and ego, the harder it is to create an authentic environment for teaching and learning for equity. *Authentic Presence for equity is the act of releasing negativity and clearing space for the birth of a counter-narrative.*

Being vulnerable in front of students can be terrifying. This fear became evident while coaching a white, gay, male teacher in a high school that serviced majority black and brown students. I was there as a consultant to support teachers with infusing their Advisory program with social justice pedagogy. This particular teacher wanted us to focus our work on how he could improve engagement in his classroom, especially around literature that referenced race and racism. As I came to know more about him, the school and the students, I suggested that perhaps he not start with a text or a discussion about racism, that he should work in other ways to build trust. When he asked how he might be able to do that, I proposed he share a text about being gay and perhaps share a personal story about his own experience being gay. He immediately felt put off by my idea. He explained his sexual orientation was private and has nothing to do with his work as a teacher. I pointed out that a group of LGBT students had recently submitted a proposal to the principal to start a support network and club because many of the gay students were experiencing bullying at recess and in the community. I told him that his willingness to address a sensitive topic that directly related to his own experience would go a long way in building trust as well as demonstrating how learning can be relevant to what was is going on with the students outside the classroom. The teacher's face got red and hard. He demanded to know why he couldn't just get to the topic of race and racism. So I asked, "How do you think the students might feel being asked to share their thoughts about race and racism in a space controlled by a white male teacher?" The teacher thought about this and in the long pause, I knew I had made a point. Unfortunately, this teacher chose not to expose his vulnerability and instead, kept pushing me to help him with his agenda to encourage his students speak to him about race and racism.

Revealing Your True Self in Service of Others

Arriving at such a willingness to expose your true self to others, including what makes you feel most vulnerable, is not easy, especially in a world that that teaches us that power and privilege are part of the natural world order and those who subscribe to this worldview are rewarded. It takes time, daily effort, study and surrounding yourself with like-minded individuals. I have found that many teachers choose the practice of yoga, meditation or mindfulness as a way to distance themselves from the material world, from ego, from thoughts and distractions. This certainly has the power and potential to build greater self-awareness, social awareness and mindfulness practices. Meditation helps us to break down false notions of "otherness" and reconnects us to our creative life source that honors all people on earth as being interconnected. However, I have found that the practice of yoga, meditation and even mindfulness are not always enough.

In the research for this book, I interviewed author and Australian scholar Edwin Ng, who wrote the book *Buddhism and Cultural Studies: A Profession of Faith*. His article entitled "Mindfulness and Social Justice: Planting the Seeds of a More Compassionate Future" had a great impact on me because he addresses what I had been observing in my work with educators, that many who are fluent in the language of "mindfulness" do not always exhibit agency for equity nor actively engage in social justice pedagogy. In his article he writes:

> *Mindfulness has entered these sites primarily as a mode of stress intervention, an effective way to help individuals maintain personal wellbeing as they perform their duties under duress. It is unquestionably important to help individuals foster mental health and wellbeing. But the stresses of contemporary living are not simply a problem of the individual. It is also undoubtedly important to interrogate and intervene in the structural conditions that generate stress in the first place, especially if these conditions continue to benefit from and perpetuate systemic inequality, exploitation and injustice, privileging some at the expense of others.[8]*

In our interview, I wanted to explore this idea further. Is mindfulness solely an individual therapeutic practice even though through mindfulness and meditation many individuals contend that they experience a heightened Spirit Consciousness? If so, how do we connect mindfulness (and by extension Spirit Consciousness) to agency for equity? In response to my inquiry, Edwin explained, "The 2011 special issue of *Contemporary Buddhism* on mindfulness features an exchange between Jon Kabat-Zinn and Buddhist scholars and teachers. In his paper for the issue, Bhikkhu Bodhi notes that the Mindfulness-Based Stress Reduction's definition of mindfulness as 'non-judgmental awareness' does not take into account the supporting role of other aspects of mindfulness training such as ardency (ātāpī), appropriate attention (yoniso manasikarā), and clear comprehension (sampajañña). For Bhikkhu Bodhi, critical awareness of systemic and structural forces of domination, and discerning acts of 'conscientious compassion,' would fall under the domain of clear comprehension; 'non-judgmental awareness' alone does not cultivate these."

Edwin continued on to say, "This is an example to show that mindfulness can be used therapeutically to help individuals manage their personal wellbeing but there is a risk that an individualistic and therapeutic approach to mindfulness becomes coopted by the status quo as an apparatus of discipline and control, whereby systemic and structural problems are reduced to personal shortcomings. What I and others like me propose as 'critical mindfulness' is therefore a more expansive approach to mindfulness that includes within its purview an interrogation of the broader social, cultural, political, economic, and ideological conditions under which the individualistic, therapeutic mindfulness has become so popular. We know, for example, that racism and discrimination cannot be reduced to the personal shortcomings of individuals. Rather, they are historically conditioned and embedded in social norms and structures."

In my dialogue with Edwin, I was better able to understand how a teacher might practice meditation and mindfulness, but still struggle with acting in ways that are equitable or that further equitable social arrangements. Buddhist mindfulness must be understood as a way to end suffering, but not only one's individual or personal suffering, but *the causes of suffering*. So, if we are to connect this to what we know about agency for equity, Authentic Presence is not mindfulness and meditation (although these practices certainly lead to it) but rather it is the act of investing in one's inner work in order to change behavior in the world, always keeping the value of all life at our center. Through mindfulness and meditation, we do come to a deeper awareness of our interdependence and Oneness. We dissolve our ego and therefore begin to understand the value of all life. We also become aware of suffering and the causes of suffering. These are all the drivers behind agency for equity, but we still have to ask ourselves, what do we do with this awareness, this knowing? How do we take critical mindful action in the world to make a difference that matters? How do we reduce our own suffering *and* the suffering of others?

Fundamental to understanding Authentic Presence is to see it as part of this engagement praxis, that is to be in relationship and dialogue with others. This should happen across race, class, ethnicity, gender, sexual orientation and so on. In relationship and through dialogue, we reveal ourselves with truth and honesty and we begin to refine our awareness to include the reality that any notion of "self" as different or separate than "other" is an illusion. In building reciprocity in relationship and dialogue with others, we come to know and experience Oneness.

It is important to understand that meditation and mindfulness practices are about how we focus our attention on our breath, for example. In this attention, we can slow down time, alter our state and enter into a more expansive space in which we lose our sense of self vs. other. This is the pathway through which we can then begin to build communion with other human beings. Our attention on breath allows for a departure from thoughts that are often adopted from a socially constructed world, not our authentic self. This stillness or silencing of thoughts provides us with an entry point to experience a spiritual connection with others. It is similar to the act of prayer, when from a clear mind, we can bring into our thoughts a person we care deeply about and pray for his or her health and well-being. We can only make space for others if we are completely free from our own suffering.

Authentic Presence emerges when we make a commitment to do both the inner work and the outer work, the former being a meditational practice and the latter being our engagement with others in intentional dialogue. Awareness and mediation lead to the falling away of the illusion of self as separate from others which is the pathway through which we can begin to channel our energy into deep listening and communication. Equitable social arrangements arise when we fully see and treat others as if they are a reflection of ourselves.

Authentic Presence, which I describe as the practice of integrating the mind, body and Spirit Consciousness in order to *communicate purpose and inspire is a creative act* that requires both a cleared mind and the commitment to engagement with others and dialogue. Without engagement, we are trapped inside ourselves, which is not Oneness nor love. If we are to consider Authentic Presence as a practice for teachers, then we must provide teachers with the time for individual, meditational and mindfulness practices *and* provide them with a safe space for authentic dialogue with others across race, class, gender, etc. If we do not address these two things in teacher education, then our work for equity will always fall into the void of good intentions.

Unpeeling the Onion by Design

Let me share a story. Many years ago my organization was hosting a conference for teachers and administrators in Boston. An African-American veteran principal who was involved in the civil rights movement stood up in the middle of a session and pointed his finger at the young white woman sitting across from him. "You don't see color? You don't see color? If you don't see color you don't see me!" His voice thundered and shook the room. The young white girl looked shocked at first but then broke down and cried. She mumbled something to the effect of, "I'm just trying to say I love all children the same!" All of the participants looked at the old black man horrified while the young girl's "white" tears engendered compassion as evidenced by several white participants close to her table who got up and gathered around her to comfort her. The old black man walked out of the room, stoic and alone.

At first glance, one might ask, why was he so angry? Why did he scream at her at what was meant to be a professional learning opportunity? But, if we suspend judgment and dig a little deeper, we would discover that this was not this educator's first conference but in fact he had been required to attend many conferences in his career purportedly designed to help principals like himself "turn around" low-performing schools that serve primarily poor, black and brown students. Just like all the others, there was no space designed for any formalized discussion of race, class, culture, access or equity

> We must clear the space, not only within our minds but outside in our collective presence, to allow new air in, to breathe together and interact, to allow for the imperfect dialogue, so that in the very least, we learn that each of us is somewhere on this shaky journey of working for peace and healing.

on the agenda. Instead educators were forced into circles and asked to discuss how to close achievement gaps, which again, makes the black student a gap that needs to be fixed. The hosts of the conference (of which I was a part) were not responsive to the wide range of social, historical and political legacies brought into the room. This thoughtlessness, which in this principal's opinion was all too typical, was bound to create tensions. Both the gentleman and the young teacher were responding to what I call the Pressure Cooker Effect. Authentic Presence is not an individual practice, but rather we as educators must take our inner work and provide multiple opportunities for ourselves and others to engage in dialogue, to co-exist, to bring out the silence of suffering and bring light to the shadows of our practice. We must clear the space, not only within our minds but outside in our collective presence, to allow new air in, to breathe together and interact, to allow for the imperfect dialogue, so that in the very least, we learn that each of us is somewhere on this shaky journey of working for peace and healing.

We are all perfectly designed and organized into situations and relationships that help us to do this work together, to begin the process of integrating our mind, body and Spirit Consciousness in such a way that we will eventually find ways to communicate a shared purpose and inspire others. Educators who are on the road to Authentic Presence make lots of mistakes. It is scary to meditate at first and find all these thoughts clouding our space; similarly, it can be terrifying to enter into dialogue across race and class. In the process of heightening one's awareness, one might accidentally intrude on the other. Sorry, did I offend you? I am so sorry, you might say, I'm just so awkward and uncomfortable right now and I know what I am saying must sound all over the place and horrible even. I am willing to stay here with you and get it right. Authentic Presence inspires through willingness to be vulnerable and it's a public commitment to purpose. The work is not about you, it is about you allowing yourself to be absorbed into the evolution of the world.

Awareness can be liberating and also very tricky. How we use language and words to communicate meaning, how our relationships define who we are and what we think is important, how we choose to channel our energy—all of this is an evolving awareness and how we respond to life situations will depend on where we are on our path to Conscientious Engagement. The more aware you are of the totality and fluidity of one's culture and identity, the more you are free to rid yourself and others from it.

For educators that work in less diverse contexts, the practice of Authentic Presence with equity in mind has its unique set of challenges. As a result of the unsettling Trump campaign, his election to presidency and his appointments into government, there has been an increase in hate crimes, bullying and public demonstrations of white, Christian supremacy and nationalism. Teachers and those who support them will have to ask themselves, how does this impact our work and the role of the teacher? How can teachers model and teach Authentic Presence in such a harmful, crowded world space? Howard Zinn, historian, educator, activist and author of the *People's History of the United States*, argued that teaching and politics are inextricable. In an interview with Amy Goodman, Zinn explains, "I don't believe it's possible to be neutral. The world is already moving in certain directions. And to be neutral, to be passive in a situation like that is to collaborate with whatever is going on. And I, as a teacher, do not want to be a collaborator with whatever is happening in the world. I want myself, as a teacher, and I want you as students, to intercede with whatever is happening in the world."[9]

Overcoming Obstacles to Authentic Presence

I have found that there are codes of behavior that adults adhere to out of fear that act as a barrier to authenticity and presence. Adults want to belong and fit in, just like children. I will talk in depth about this in the next chapter, but for now, suffice it to say that adults want to feel good about themselves, good about their relationshops and the work they do. However Authentic Presence will be threatened if adults become fearful of losing status within an organization or if they are concerned about job security. Adults have a lot to lose; we have responsibilities like raising families, paying the bills and taking care of aging parents, so adults easily become guarded and protect themselves against possible (or imagined) vulnerabilities to their personal well-being. This narrow focus on self, and fear of survival works against Authentic Presence in that Authentic Presence requires that we are open and vulnerable in front of others. It is about honesty and engaging in authentic dialogue with others regardless of one's role within an organization. Exposing yourself, standing up for what you believe in and asking questions that may challenge normative thinking may have consequences. That is why Authentic Presence requires structures that protect individuals from getting fired, harassed or discriminated against by their colleagues. Unfortunately, in my experience, there is little trust, across race, gender, religion and class and not many structures put in place to protect people from abuses, especially since they are really hard to explain and quantify. There are very real reasons that teachers and teacher educators shut down authentic work and do the bare minimum on the job rather than act in the best interest of equity. Conscientious Engagement is hard, revolutionary work. In agreeing to engage conscientiously, you are essentially saying that you are going to build the capacity in yourself and others to be open and vulnerable, honest and authentic in a climate where fear, deception, power and ego dominate our collective space.

Several years ago, I worked with a team on a three-year whole-school transformation project. Part of my job was to facilitate team meetings, model the use of protocols and help the school build a professional community of inquiry. One team included a veteran educator who was the union rep for the school. She was outspoken and many of her peers considered her wise and even a good teacher. She was extremely critical of my role and rightly so. All transformation projects are political and in this case, the integrity of our company and the price tag on our service in a district servicing poor students of color was questionable. She attended the mandatory team meetings regularly but bulldozed several of my efforts to keep to the protocols by either dominating the conversation or responding to any innovative thinking with negativity.

I identified with this veteran teacher. I appreciated her resistance and her voice. As a result, I struggled with Authentic Presence in my current role. In another life, I thought, she would be me. Yet, I was also appalled at the overall conditions and climate of the schools in the district. The lack of urgency around changing teaching practices and engaging the students, who were majority Latino, was negligent. There was no parent and community involvement and no reflection of the wealth of culture and community in the building, reading and math scores were dismal, there were no alternative assessments and the bilingual services for ELLs were archaic in spite of the fact that the majority of the kids spoke Spanish in their homes. Teachers were for the most part complacent and held very low expectations for the children.

I had to stop and ask myself: Why am I here? What is the most important thing? How can I communicate a sense of urgency while finding compassion for their everyday practice? These questions and my meditation on them became so important throughout my time there.

During one meeting the veteran teacher (and union rep) became especially animated and negative when I proposed the need to reconsider the curriculum, which was not aligned to the standards. I found myself at a crossroads in my practice. I had to do something or else I was going to lose them and our work would go nowhere. I breathed in and out, in and out and then, finally took a risk. I began to share my own personal reservations about my role as an education consultant and even this notion of "transformation." I acknowledged that many for-profit companies were pillaging poor school districts in the country and many of them really didn't care about the children. I also shared my respect and regard for the role of unions in our country as a way to protect the rights of employees and especially as a way to protect the rights and needs of women within the profession. I validated the teacher's feelings that often new "protocols" in team meetings might appear meaningless and abstract when everyday reality consisted of combating depression, trying to figure out how to manage recalcitrant and/or apathetic youth, staying in compliance, pushing more testing on already disengaged, low-performing students, navigating the rapid changes in the school's leadership and teaching with few resources.

As I listed all the reasons for her to be angry, I felt a wave of emotion in my voice as I connected deeply with the teachers' suffering, which was also my suffering, and the feeling of impotence that none of us really has the power to do anything about. I felt the passion of my words pour out of me and in these moments, I felt a shift in the energy in the room as if suddenly the teachers realized that I too was human, riddled with contradictions, and that we were together in the mess of it. By unraveling and challenging my role and juxtaposing it with my "inner self" in such a public way, I demonstrated how fragile and subject to interrogation we all are.

When I finished, there was a silence in the room. But the energy was palpable.

Then, I asked: But now that I have said all this, can you honestly say that you think the children in this school are getting a good, solid education? Do you think they have a fighting chance to make something of themselves in the world when they graduate?

Silence.

I looked at the English teacher and asked: How many writers and journalists are going to come from this institution? How many books will we find in the bookstore written by the hand of one of your students?

Silence.

There is something wrong here, isn't there? So, is there anything at all that we can we do differently? Anything at all?

Silence.

No one could argue the fact that the students were not getting a quality education. But what could we do? What was the change going to be?

Shockingly, the meeting came alive! There was an outburst of comments and thoughts and questions. There was still discomfort, but now it was the discomfort of inaction. It was such an important shift and I had not yet experienced it until that very moment.

Later when I was on the three-hour train ride back home, I thought long and hard about my practice of Authentic Presence.

I had exposed myself, the contradictions of my role as a transformation consultant and the work in that context. I contemplated all of the dynamics and the relationships. I examined my loyalties to my self, to equity, to the teachers and to my company. Had I responded in the right way? A gentleman who sat across from me on the train broke into my thoughts.

He asked, "Are you a professor at Brown University?"
"No," I replied, "Why do you ask?"
"Oh, I just get that feeling."

Strangely, my Conscientious Educator self had emanated outward. He continued on to say he was a psychologist and we began to discuss his work, which was fascinating. Within no time at all, I felt comfortable to share my own story and my personal dilemma around the practice of Authentic Presence. After listening intently, he smiled and reassured me that I had fully honored the moment in the best way possible. He pointed out that the fact that I was still contemplating on it, going over all the detail in my mind, trying on each point of view, suggested that I was Authentic and Present. "You care so deeply about the work," he said matter-of-factly. And that's when I exhaled. A stranger on the train put in my path to validate the power of Authentic Presence, once again.

As it turns out, my strange and colorful spiraling light I call my Angel visited me shortly after that episode and soon thereafter, I would learn that my work with that company would come to a bitter end. After successfully gaining the trust of many of the teachers at the school (the union rep stayed distant, however, and ended up submitting her paperwork for retirement) and opening the way for full "co-ownership" of our program, which included a wonderful Lesson Study protocol, I was later accused of being disloyal to my company's CEO and his values. It was yet another experience that highlighted the great paradox of my life as a change agent.

Authentic Presence, for all of us, regardless of your earthbound identity, can be difficult, painful and lonely work. Yet, it is the only way that doesn't fail to provide us warriors with what we are truly working for—and that is the expression of love, creativity and the inner peace that we are making a difference in the lives of others that matters.

Reflection Questions

1. How might you begin to raise Consciousness of the nature of your thoughts? What thoughts do you feel shame or guilt about? Where do you think these thoughts come from? How would you feel if your mind were rid of them?
2. When did you last make yourself vulnerable in front of someone or a group? What was the response? What was your motivation for making yourself vulnerable?
3. What might happen if you spoke up against the norms or challenged consensus in your school or organization?
4. What steps can you take that will engage you in the practice of Authentic Presence?

Notes

1. Namaste Holistic Healing and Yoga Center. Namaste defined. Available online at: http://namastetruckee.com/namaste-defined
2. Newberg, A. (2014). *The Metaphysical Mind: Probing the Biology of Philosophical Thought*. CreateSpace Publishing.
3. Dunne, J. (1993). *Back to the Rough Ground : 'Phronesis' and 'Techne' in Modern Philosophy and in Aristotle*. Notre Dame: University of Notre Dame Press.
4. Kornelsen, L. (2006). Teaching with presence. In P. Cranton (ed.), *Authenticity in Teaching: New Directions for Adult and Continuing Education*. San Francisco: Jossey Bass, pp. 73–82.
5. Cranton, P. (2001). *Becoming an Authentic Teacher in Higher Education*. Malabar, FL: Krieger.
6. Cranton, P. & Carusetta E. (2004). Perspectives on authenticity in teaching. *Adult Education Quarterly*, Vol. 55, No. 1, pp. 5–22.

7. Cited in Dirkx, J.M. (2006). Authenticity and imagination. In P. Cranton (ed.). *Authenticity in Teaching: New Directions for Adult and Continuing Education.*

8. Ng, E. (2015). Mindfulness and social justice: Planting the seeds of a more compassionate future. ABC Religion and Ethics. Available online at: http://www.abc.net.au/religion/articles/2015/06/29/426 4094.htm

9. Democracy Now (2005). Howard Zinn: "To Be neutral, to be passive in a situation is to collaborate with whatever is going on." April 27. Available online at: https://www.democracynow.org/2005/4/27/howard_zinn_to_be_neutral_to

8

Entanglement

3. **Entanglement** (We are entangled with some people more than others and these relationships impact how we behave in the world)

"The perennial destiny of principles: while everyone professes to have them, they are likely to be sacrificed when they become inconveniencing. Generally a moral principle is something that puts one at variance with accepted practice. And that variance has consequences, sometimes unpleasant consequences, as the community takes its revenge on those who challenge its contradictions—who want a society actually to uphold the principles it professes to defend."
Susan Sontag, *Of Courage and Resistance*, 2013

Love is quantifiable and so are the social and emotional commitments we have to those people we identify with and who form part of our inner circle. Individuals in our inner circle are there because of a shared identity. Identity can be attributed to one's gender, race, religion, social class or ethnic origin. It could also be a profession (doctor, teacher, homemaker) or political affiliation such as Democrat, Republican or Independent. However we choose to identify ourselves, we inevitably look to identity as a built-in kinship with some people. With some, we share a common history, heritage, language or ideology. Our allegiance to group or social identities informs our outlook on life and how we engage with the people. It also informs how those outside our "circle" see us. This is fundamental to understanding Entanglement, which states we are entangled with some people and these relationships do impact our behavior in the world.

An Entangling Situation

A few years ago, I had the opportunity to work in Puerto Rico as an education consultant. The idea of working on the island of my ancestors was extremely attractive to me. Puerto Rican heritage has always been a part of my identity. I believed that living and working there would provide me with insights into myself and my people that could inspire a new way of approaching education for Puerto Ricans, who often struggle in traditional US public school settings. I got involved with a small firm that was hired to help the Puerto Rican government train and support English teachers on the new English language curriculum that was in many ways similar to the Common Core and the Understanding by Design model of instruction. The reform effort there was ambitious. The new curriculum was given to teachers just a few short weeks before the beginning of the school year with the expectation that they would implement it right away without sufficient training, if any. The curriculum was online, a format that required that teachers spend a few hundred dollars of their own money printing out the materials. Otherwise, they would need access to a computer with secure Internet access, neither of which is a guarantee for teachers in Puerto Rico, especially in the public schools. When I arrived at a school at the bottom of a mountain, the principal had no idea that I was contracted to work there. Even more troubling were the significant gaps in oral English proficiency skills and pedagogy amongst the teachers I was charged with supporting.

When I approached my colleagues at their office in San Juan, they shirked any responsibility. They explained districts are unorganized. They devalued the role of technology and dismissed my concerns that the expectations for teachers were unrealistic. They handed me a stack of forms to fill out so I could get paid, offered me several links to websites and sent me on my way.

In short time, I met a teacher who received me into his classroom with open arms. He schooled me about the politics on the island. One detail I remember learning from him was teacher interviews and resumes often included reference to a political affiliation, which would either help or hinder a candidate. He spoke at great length about the injustice of district officials who partnered with for-profit companies who under the guise of reform took advantage of poor districts. I became embarrassed, to say the least, that I was working for one of these companies. What was I supposed to do now? I wondered. I wanted and needed the work and was set on working in Puerto Rico. I had always considered myself a "free agent" but it became increasingly clear that I was not. Seeing the look of consternation of my face, the teacher told me about a man who had a good reputation in the education community. This man, he told me, had built a life in service of the people, not like these crooks, as he called them. This man came from very humble beginnings. With great resolve he had earned a doctorate degree, and with his learning and experience working with the education department, he started a not-for-profit organization to improve the life of his people through quality education. Eventually, he expanded his vision to open his own school that he built on top of a mountain. I was intrigued and inspired by this man's story and the level of energy with which this teacher described him to me. My inner sonar was alerted. I was drawn to this individual. How would I be able to disentangle myself from my current working relationships and still work in Puerto Rico?

Group Membership and Social Situations

The insights learned from social identity theory confirm that the groups to which people belong mean something to them.[1] Social identity theory was developed by Henri Tajfel and John Turner to understand the psychological basis for intergroup

discrimination.[2] The basic prediction inherent in this theory is
that group membership will produce discrimination that favors
the in-group at the expense of the out-group.[3] Although there
have been numerous studies aimed at deepening our understanding of social identity theory, there seems to be consistent
evidence to indicate that group membership does profoundly
affect individuals in social situations. Why would we expect differently? Do you believe human beings extend the word "family"
to just anybody? If you and I are in relationship with one another
because we are family, how can that not distinguish our relationship as being unique, as compared to someone who is not part of
this association called "family"? Human beings will instinctively
favor some more than others. They will also not trust everybody
in the same way. From early on, we tell children, "Don't talk to
strangers." We pass on from generation to generation this integral
wisdom that is part of our survival instinct. Similarly, we do not
extend the benefits of trust, the level of care and concern we offer
to those in our inner circle. We trust and care for our own as best
we can and with the resources at our disposal. Understanding
these elements of human behavior, without judgments, can be
liberating, especially when we are often told that equity is about
treating everyone the same. Perhaps how we frame our work for
equity contradicts the human condition and even most people's
common sense.

If we want to develop agency for equity, we need to examine this notion of 'affirming diversity' made very popular by
Prof. Sonia Nieto and consider how often diversity and equity
can create conflict and cognitive dissonance within our psyches.
Diversity, which is accepting and embracing our differences, is
considered to be a fundamental part of equity work. While noble
in cause, diversity initiatives have become faddish and in education circles diversity has been reduced to a form of political
correctness. The political correctness that governs much of our
behavior in education is based on the premise that public expressions of loyalty to a social group are wrong because they lead
to abuse of power. Therefore, in the world of political correctness, public acknowledgment of preferences for some or having
any group affinity, whether through words or action, may be

considered suspect of nepotism, prejudice or bias. As a result, educators are careful with what they reveal when in the presence of some audiences. Group affiliations and/or associations to certain people are conveniently left out of conversations. Educators adeptly use language and words in the public space to suggest neutrality and an ideology that "everybody is the same." And yet, in private spaces, educators, like everyone else, have their group affiliations and allegiances, which in some cases espouse ideologies that are far from neutral, nor are they particularly tolerant to those outside the group membership. A perfect case in point is the controversy surrounding the relationship between President Trump and Stephen Bannon.

Can We Separate the Personal from the Professional?

Notions of diversity and equity in this light can be seen as compartmentalized or a double standard. Ideological stances around equity and diversity as expressed through our language and other behaviors are reserved for the professional space and public discourse but don't necessarily apply to our personal space. Is it possible for educators to affirm diversity, to see and treat everybody the same in the professional space while having very strong ties to individuals or groups who think and behave differently in the private/personal space? Also, is it possible in the field of education in particular, when our job involves the care and treatment of human beings, to separate personal ideologies from professional ideologies? In other words, is it possible that our relationships, church affiliations, religious beliefs, friendship groups, political affiliations, club memberships and so on *do not* influence how we behave in the school space, how we treat and respond to colleagues, children and families?

Evidence indicates that we are greatly influenced by group membership and our rational or politically correct behaviors that may affirm and/or embrace diversity can be a source of cognitive dissonance. This can be a barrier to agency for equity. In my experience, many educators in the neoliberal sphere where funding and lobbying becomes part of the day-to-day work in service of public education have become expert at the art of deception. We do not (nor are we really expected to) bring our "whole" selves to our work because in many cases if we reveal our entangled relationships and/or group affiliations, we would put into question who we really are and what we value. Pretending that we don't feel a natural kinship to members of our group or that social group identity does not influence our behavior makes it very difficult if not impossible for educators to practice Conscientious Engagement, because Conscientious Engagement is about living what Palmer Parker calls an undivided life.[4] Being a conscientious educator does not mean you are a stranger to group affiliations or identity preferences; it means that you are acutely aware of them and how they function. It means you make a decision to engage in the every day practice of the examination of self, including your thoughts, your actions, your feelings and how you channel energy. In this way you make a commitment to transcend your human proclivities and embrace practices aligned with a Spirit Consciousness.

In the moving speech Susan Sontag delivered at Rothko Chapel in Houston in response to the Israeli soldiers' movement for selective refusal to serve in the occupied territories, she said:

> To fall out of step with one's tribe; to step beyond one's tribe into a world that is larger mentally but smaller numerically—if alienation or dissidence is not your habitual or gratifying posture, this is a complex, difficult process. It is hard to defy the wisdom of the tribe, the wisdom that values the lives of members of the tribe above all others. It will always be unpopular—it will always be deemed unpatriotic—to say that the lives of the members of the other tribe are as valuable as one's own. It is easier to give one's allegiance to those we know, to those we see, to those with whom we are embedded, to those with whom we share—as we may—a community of fear.[5]

My experience in Puerto Rico was one of many life lessons about the nature of tribes and entangled relationships and how they impact our decisions in education. As much as Americans try to pretend they don't exist, our entanglements can either help or hinder our work for equity. We do not grow up into the world as "free agents." We are not free of associations, free of entangled relationships, free of the constraints imposed on us by way of our roles and responsibilities in society. Perhaps we are born free, but we are not by default *free* in life insofar as we belong to and function in society, which is an organized web of intricate entangled relationships. I posit that you do have a choice, however, as to the type of relationships that you keep that define your commitment to equity. There is always a choice to move further into Spirit Consciousness, where all walks of life, no matter what social group you belong to, are respected and honored with equal reverence.

So, it is true, you will never *see* everybody the same in the professional workspace because we are human beings first and human beings live in society in which we are simply all *not* the same. We are all different and although we all share the fundamental characteristics of being human, we each have a unique cultural history and worldview, all of which I discussed in previous chapters. However, like I said, it is possible to treat and respond to every living human being equally with love and fairness through Spirit Consciousness. Spirit Consciousness is the medium through which human beings may rise above the duality of Mind and Body and enter the realm of universal wisdom and love and liberation from the dictates of ego. Without Spirit Consciousness, behavior is driven by the duality of a segregated mind, which is where bias lives and other antithetical human proclivities and dispositions. Spirit Consciousness allows humans to tap into an enormous frequency that energizes the "wholeness" of being, which transcends identity and any false ideologies that get reinforced through shared reality, such as our separateness, superiority or missionary mentality. This transcendence results in a new, evolutionary Being that is able to treat and respond to every human being with love, non-violence and fairness and it also enables us to attract other Beings who may not belong to our traditional networks or inner circles, but who share in the same life purpose.

Being Aware of Your Entangled Relationships

In the practice of Conscientious Engagement, new entangled relationships are born out of Spirit Consciousness, which because of their alignment to your life purpose, will produce an abundance of creative energy, the level of energy needed to have courage, to fight for what matters, to stay involved in the most important social movement of our time. Conversely, relationships that are not in alignment with your life's purpose will continue to vibrate low energy levels and in some cases, dissipate your energy resources in such a way that you will fall into apathy or inertia. This is why some relationship dynamics, collaborative groups, or committees, for example, may feel toxic and leave us feeling worn out and tired all the time, rather than inspired. It is important to remember that agency for equity requires that we conserve and protect our energy so that we can channel it only in ways that will further our goals. I will talk more about energy in the chapter on Emergence, but for now, understand that different relationships metabolize energy in different ways.

Understanding which relationships dominate your world and how they impact your decisions and energy is part of this work. Becoming aware of and taking responsibility for your natural tendencies to stay comfortable in entangled relationships because of a sense of belonging is the first step. Even the first step alone can help to avert inertia or being implicated in the abuse of power through bias. It may sound like a paradox, but only through understanding our entangled relationships and how they impact our behavior can we transcend them in such a way that leads us to Freedom. Let us explore our social bonds and how they function.

Human beings will go to great lengths and use a variety of strategies to form and to maintain social bonds with others.[6] All human beings need to feel a sense of belonging. Belonging according to Maslow is a very basic need, right after food, water and safety. We want to know that we are understood, that when we interact with others we make sense. We do not want to feel alone. This self-affirming quality of relationships is a key driver in everything we do. Many believe the ultimate purpose of all relationships is to do reflective, soul work—where the other is a mirror for yourself so that you can reflect on and alter the image accordingly so that you can get closer to your true self, your soul self, that which radiates love. According to shared reality theory, achieving a sense of perceived mutual understanding is a potent basis of social bonds.[7,8,9]

Wan, Torelli and Chiu contend that shared reality is the totality of the knowledge that is assumed to be known and shared by others. Normative shared reality refers to the collective beliefs about the values that are widely shared among members of a group.[10] When we are entangled with another human being or with a group, we are participants in the creation of a shared reality, which may or may not be normative in nature when compared to the larger society. For example, in a school you may be entangled with a group of teachers in your building. As part of an entangled group, the shared reality will actualize itself as a core belief such as *all students can meet standards regardless of their zip code if they have a good teacher in the classroom*. The shared reality of a group of teachers is not always the nationally dominant narrative; however, in my experience, this is usually the case. Public school teachers are particularly susceptible because narratives that aim to define the role of public education in America and the role of the teacher are all reinforced through politics, media, university research and development initiatives that are funded by the same government and corporations and likewise, higher education and professional development opportunities.

Shared reality determines behaviors of individuals as well as how the individuals behave with each other when working collaboratively. For example, if the shared reality around student achievement is *all students can meet standards regardless of their zip code if they have a good teacher in the classroom*, each individual will prioritize efforts on improving instructional practices (sometimes to the exclusion of all else) in spite of evidence that suggests other variables are impacting student achievement—such as lack of resources, ineffective leadership or chronic malnutrition, for example. In group settings, members who contribute findings that reinforce the prevailing shared belief receive public recognition and applause. Similarly, in a group setting, evidence presented to the contrary may be received kindly as a sign of political correctness, but systematically devalued by way of actions such as refocusing the conversation, circling back to the agenda, relegating it *outside the sphere of influence* or putting it on a list for future exploration (often requiring volunteering extra time and resources outside of the normal workday). Over time, through constant group reinforcement or devaluation, the shared reality is reified by repetition, until it becomes simply *knowledge*. This is the process of "normalization." This does not mean the group does not collaborate and create together, it just means the goal of all collaboration becomes about moving ahead fixed items on the agenda rather than questioning the agenda itself; that is, are we sure we want to invest *all of* our time and resources on teacher effectiveness?

In a study on intersubjectivity and the maintainence of normative shared reality, it was demonstrated that shared information in the group is discussed more and is given more weight in the group's decision than unshared information."[11] In the communication chain, information that is consistent with the shared reality often perpetuates through information transmission whereas information that is inconsistent with it tends to drop out in the process.[12] When widely circulated narrative content is consistent with the normative shared reality, it is evaluated in cultural terms—the more the protagonist in the narrative is seen as a representative of the culture, the more favorably the protagonist will be evaluated. The shared reality functions to maintain positive social relationships between people who share the reality in the relationship,[13,14] therefore betrayal of normative shared reality threatens people's relationship with the group.[15] I have encountered numerous times working with schools and education organizations many creative, innovative or independent thinkers who have acquiesced to the demands of the job and have mastered the art of "normalcy" within group dynamics, thereby suppressing the voice of their authentic self.

When individual members of entangled groups choose to live divided lives because they are motivated to maintain positive social relations compounded with the fear of losing a job, agency for equity dies. While the individual may have enough strength to nurture and independently develop innovative ideas that often have the potential to revolutionize how we do schooling, individuals will reach a point in which they realize that a community of like-minded souls is needed in order to move these "seed" ideas into the larger socio-political and cultural landscape. Innovative ideas need to be shaped and molded into a language that is shared so that it can result in a salient and cohesive counter-narrative. Further, the physical, intellectual and spiritual demands imposed upon individuals who feel trapped in a divided life cycle are enormous and their health and long-term commitment to equity is threatened. The amount of energy it takes to appeal to group norms and applaud a counter-creative shared reality (one that does not move in alignment with our evolutionary Spirit Consciousness) should not be underestimated. It becomes incumbent upon the evolutionary teacher and change agent for equity to conserve and channel all energy for the integration of new ideas towards the building of an egalitarian society. This we know from the wisdom of the ages; we must constantly evolve and change or else we perish.

Here is a quote from a professor who is becoming aware of this dynamic:

> *I have changed my mind about the power of institutional and situational constraints and have become much more aware of the potential such constraints have—especially when they are not consciously recognized or explicitly stated—to shape our behavior and prevent us from acting consistently with our own most important priorities, and further to hide from us by habituation the extent to which our behavior has ceased to be consistent with our own fundamental convictions.*[16]

Getting informed and familiarizing oneself with prevailing social forces and dominant narratives that continue to shape our collective, shared reality and by extension, our group identity, as teachers is important to the process of Conscientious Engagement. Entanglements that are built around shared identities such as gender, race, ethnicity, sexual orientation, spirituality, religion, political affiliation and so on do a good job in "hiding from us by habituation," the very ways behavior within professional learning groups prevents us from working in alignment with our Spirit Consciousness. This is what many call "identity politics," including Dr. Cornell West, who speaks at length about this being a threat to our work for equity. An example of this is when we choose a black male or a lesbian for a leadership position, but their political platform and ideologies actually suppress the right of people of color or discriminate because of sexual orientation.

Implications for Teaching

For teachers in particular, we should be aware that we have collectively agreed to accept and maintain the dominant narrative or shared reality that *knowledge is a commodity*. Knowledge is a commodity means it can be taken or given, sold or bought, controlled by market forces. Knowledge is a commodity has philosophical underpinnings in the nature of man (Darwinism) and by extension, how we define our economic and political system—capitalism. In this paradigm, knowledge and, by extension, intelligence is deemed to have a value structure that can be assigned a price, often attached to certain educational institutions and degrees. The value of knowledge can be adjusted accordingly, just like the market, but there are always in a hegemonic society fixed values that we call a "classical" education. Knowledge obtained from a community college, for example, is less valuable than a degree from Harvard University. Any knowledge that lives outside of this structure—such as autodidacticism, online and independent study programs, home schooling, knowledge obtained from life experience, knowledge attached to indigenous cultures—is determined to have a lesser value or is simply marginalized or an anomaly.

Another shared reality that teachers tend to uphold in group settings is that performance on standardized tests equates to intelligence. Although there is substantial research that indicates that performance on tests is largely predicated on economic status and the education attainment of parents, this shared reality that continues to drive education discourse and decision-making in group settings is dangerous. Jerome Bruner, professor and major architect of Head Start wrote, "We lead the world in the standard deviation of composite scores—the most diverse country in the well off world. Our lowest percentile is way down; our top tenth is way up. America seems to have a gift for fostering maldistribution or inequality. No country in the civilized world can match in terms of the maldistribution of wealth, the gap between rich and poor."[17] Wealth distribution correlates to scores and those with the least are relegated to the bottom rungs of the ladder within our social hierarchy.

Deficit theory, culture of poverty, and genetic inferiority are all ubiquitously shared realities that are often left unchallenged in group discourse. Our use of language and how we frame conversations in education reify these normative shared realities that are not based on any sound research but rather are attached to the distortion of data, scientific tools and measurements that are used precisely as a way to perpetuate deficit theories and notions of genetic inferiority. In Ansari's study of discourse and ideologies of college readiness in an urban black context, she writes:

Deficit ideologies assume that achievement is a result of innate ability (Hernstein & Murray, 1994; Jensen, 1969, 1972, 1973), cultural values, and parenting styles (Bloom, Davis, & Hess, 1965; Deutsch, 1967; Frost & Hawkes, 1966; Gottlieb & Ramsey, 1967; Lewis, 1966). In essence, the "home culture" provides inadequate support and preparation for academic success, leading to significantly lower outcomes (Barrington & Hendricks, 1989; Beck & Muia 1980; Caplan, Choy, & Whitmore, 1991; Kronik, Peterson, Morton, & Smith, 1989; Labov, 1982; Villegas, 1988). This theory assumes that middle-class values are the normative standard and that there is an inherent deficit in the cultures of minority students (Caplan et al., 1991; Labov, 1982; Villegas, 1988). The deficit ideologies are instantiated in the codes that many educators use for children of color: "at risk," "urban," and "struggling." In effect students are labeled and sorted and framed even before they even enter school. What is not considered is the role that schooling, institutions, and school practices play in sustaining the lack of equitable access and resources.[18]

The last normative shared reality I would like to point out is the notion that we live in a meritocracy. A meritocracy suggests excellent performance within the system is rewarded and social mobility is a result of personal resolve, hard work and a commitment to education. This is the foundation of our "rigor," "grit" and "growth mindset" theories. Holes in our country's meritocracy, however, have been largely exposed now that we are undergoing the effects of extreme capitalism in which there is persistent and widening inequality, low social mobility and real limits to the type of education and jobs available to working class families, regardless of race. Attainment is more and more based on subjective measures such as recommendations, résumés, writing samples, parental legacies and interviews rather than performance and hard work. According to Chris Hayes, when we say meritocracy, we really mean oligarchy. The rationale is that it is impossible to have a system that rewards performance without having a leadership/elite/ruling class emerge.[19]

As we begin to unpack the nature and functioning of our Entanglements and the normative shared realities that are iterated within our group dynamics, we begin to learn how our thoughts are often driven and affirmed by the relationships we surround ourselves with, including relationships in the home (parents, spouse, children, etc.), relationships in the community, religious institutions, political affiliations, and so on and they also are influenced by larger, broader identities such as those that I outlined that are associated with capitalism and Americanism. Unfortunately, as our country moves towards fascist tendencies, concerted messages from the media and the press, research institutions funded by the same corporations, education policy and practice and community and religious centers will all begin to mirror each other and become normalized into one shared reality that will get harder and harder to challenge. There is important work ahead of us.

Once we begin to recognize that there are real implications attached to the relationships we choose to nurture and surround ourselves with, we can begin to identify how some entanglements either threaten our work for equity and Spirit Consciousness or support it. Embracing our life's purpose as one that aims to build through education an egalitarian society in which we reduce the suffering of humanity, we can begin to disentangle ourselves from relationships that no longer serve this purpose. This is what it means to be Free. Freedom from entanglement provides us with cleared space and energy needed to follow and act upon the moral dictates of Spirit Consciousness, that which is grounded in one's life purpose, universal wisdom and divine intelligence. Freedom also clears the space for the influx of renewed sources of energy that will come from other individuals in society who are on a similar "undivided" pathway.

> Embracing our life's purpose as one that aims to build through education an egalitarian society in which we reduce the suffering of humanity, we can begin to disentangle ourselves from relationships that no longer serve this purpose.

Einstein describes this "cosmic religious feeling" as moving from individual existence that has become a sort of prison to wanting to experience the universe as a single significant whole.[20]

Remember the story I shared about working in Puerto Rico? You might be interested to know that I was able to disentangle myself from that unscrupulous company. Right after my conversation with that teacher, I got into my car rental and with the help of a map and a kind stranger who steered me in the right direction, I found Dr. Roque Diaz Tizol, the founder and president of COSEY. His beautiful school is built on the top of a mountain overlooking the whole vicinity and as fate would have it, he agreed to meet with me. In short time, I quit my job with that company and a month later, returned back to Puerto Rico, to work in partnership with Roque.

Teachers are at the epicenter of our public domain, which includes the reproduction of our dominant narratives, but they are also situated in such a way that they can drive cultural change. We are bombarded with media, politicians, philanthropists, research and data, conflicting agendas that work in concert to tell us exactly what we are supposed to think and how we should behave. We are often corralled into professional development and meetings and are expected to direct all of efforts around the implementation of curriculum and instruction that does little to challenge the dominant narratives that perpetuate inequality. What kind of courage does a teacher need to have to challenge normative discourse in the moment it takes place, when surrounded by entangled members of their professional learning communities? How can a teacher begin to redirect the conversation to topics that matter and sustain the pressure in such a way that we can break down these pernicious normative narratives that enslave us to an approach that does not work?

Arming yourself with information from alternative sources, such as independent news platforms, and surrounding yourself with people who may not be part of your inner circle but who are on a similar life journey is critical to Conscientious Engagement. Learning from others, finding their support and encouragement, sharing in the examination of our language and discourse, taking creative risks to solve old and perennial problems, and dropping out of constraining entangled relationships that no longer serve your life purpose are all behaviors that will help you build agency for equity. You are not alone. There is a whole world of evolutionary teachers waiting.

Reflection Questions

1. Who are you entangled with? What is the nature of these relationships? How would describe the ideologies that are shared within these relationships and/or groups and how are they expressed through language?
2. What do you appreciate about the people that you interact with on a daily basis? What concerns you about how they may think about the children and families you teach and serve? What is their thinking about the nature of poverty, failure and the new reform agenda?
3. Are there relationships in your life, or groups that you belong to that drain your energy? What is the dynamic of these relationships? Do you think you can effect change within these groups? How? If not, how might you begin

to disentangle yourself from these social bonds to move closer to your life's purpose?

4. What news sources, media outlets and/or newspapers do you rely on for information? Are there other resources that you can explore on topics related to education, equity or the dynamic nature of human evolution that might offer you different perspective?

5. How can you begin to create space for new relationships and ideas to manifest in your life? How might you experiment with your daily routine in ways that may expand your understanding of equity and society?

Notes

1. Chen, Y. & Li, S.X. (2009). Group identity and social preferences. The American Economic Review, Vol. 99, No. 1, pp. 431–457.

2. Tajfel, H. & Turner, J. (1979). An integrative theory of intergroup conflict. In S. Worchel & W. Austin (eds.), The Social Psychology of Intergroup Relations. Monterey, CA: Brooks/Cole, pp. 33–47.

3. Charness, G., Rigotti, L. & Rustichini, A. (2007) Individual behavior and group membership. The American Economic Review, Vol. 97, No. 4, pp. 1340–1352.

4. Palmer, P. (1998). The Courage to Teach: Exploring the Inner Landscape of a Teacher's Life. John Wiley & Sons

5. Sontag, S. (2003). Of courage and resistance: At center of our moral life are the great stories of those who have said no. The Nation, April 17. https://www.thenation.com/article/courage-and-resistance/

6. Baumeister, R. & Leary, M. (1995). The need to belong: Desire for interpersonal attachments as fundamental human motivation. Psychological Bulletin, Vol. 117, No. 3.

7. Hardin, C. D, & Conley, T. (2001). A relational approach to cognition: Shared experience and relationship affirmation in social cognition. In G. Moskowitz (ed.), Cognitive Social Psychology. Mahwah, NJ: Erlbaum, pp. 3-18.

8. Hardin, C. D. & Higgins, E. T. (1996). Shared reality: How social verification makes the subjective objective. In R. Sorrentino & E. T. Higgins (eds.), Handbook of Motivation and Cognition, Vol. 3. New York: Guilford, pp. 28–84.

9. Huntsinger, J.R. & Sinclair, S. (2010). When it feels right, go with it: Affective regulation of affiliative social tuning. *Social Cognition,* Vol. 28, No. 3, pp. 290–305.
10. Wan, C., Torelli, C. J., & Chiu, C. (2010). Intersubjective consensus and the maintenance of normative shared reality. *Social Cognition,* Vol. 28, No. 3, pp. 422–446. doi:http://dx.doi.org/10.1521/soco.2010.28.3.422
11. Stasser, G. & Stewart, D. (1992). Discovery of hidden profiles by decision-making groups: Solving a problem versus making a judgment. *Journal of Personality and Social Psychology,* Vol. 63, pp. 426–434.
12. Kashima, Y. (2000). Maintaining cultural stereotypes in the serial reproduction of narratives. *Personality and Social Psychology Bulletin,* Vol. 26, pp. 594–604.
13. Hardin, C. D, & Conley, T. (2001). A relational approach to cognition: Shared experience and relationship affirmation in social cognition. In G. Moskowitz (ed.), *Cognitive Social Psychology.* Mahwah, NJ: Erlbaum, pp. 3–18.
14. Jost, J.T., Ledgerwood, A. & Hardin, C. D. (2008). Shared reality, system justification, and the relational basis of ideological beliefs. *Social and Personality Psychology Compass,* Vol. 2, pp. 171–186.
15. Wan, C., Torelli, C. J., & Chiu, C. (2010). Intersubjective consensus and the maintenance of normative shared reality. *Social Cognition,* Vol. 28, No. 3, pp. 422–446. doi:http://dx.doi.org/10.1521/soco.2010.28.3.422
16. Hunt, R. (2006). Institutional constraints on authenticity in teaching. *New Directions for Adult and Continuing Education,* no. 111. Wiley Periodicals.
17. Bruner, J.S. (2003). Education reform. *Bulletin of the American Academy of Arts and Sciences,* LVI, pp. 48–53 (quote from p. 51).
18. Ansari, S. (2013). Deconstructing College-Readiness in an Urban Black Context: Ideology, Discourse, and Practices. Thesis. University of Illinois at Chicago.
    Hernstein, R.J., & Murray, C. (1994). *The Bell Curve.* New York, NY: Free Press.
    Jensen, A. R. (1969). How much can we boost IQ and scholastic achievement? *Harvard Educational Review,* Vol. 39, pp. 1–123.
    Jensen, A.R. (1972). *Genetics and Education.* New York, NY: Harper and Row.

Jensen, A.R. (1973). *Educability and Group Differences*. New York, NY: Harper and Row.

Bloom, B.S., Davis, A., Hess, R. (1965). *Compensatory Education for Cultural Deprivation*. New York, NY: Holt, Rinehart and Winston.

Deutsch, M. (1967). *The Disadvantaged Child*. New York, NY: Basic Books.

Frost, J. L., & Hawkes, G. R. (Eds.). (1966). *The Disadvantaged Child: Issues and Innovations*. New York, NY: Houghton Mifflin.

Gottlieb, D. & Ramsey, C. (1967). *Understanding Children of Poverty*. Chicago: Science Research and Associates.

Lewis, O. (1966). The culture of poverty. *Scientific American*, Vol. 215, No. 4, pp. 19–25.

Barrington, B. L., & Hendricks, B. (1989). Differentiating characteristics of high school graduates, dropouts, and nongraduates. *Education and Urban Society*, Vol. 82, No. 6, pp. 309–319.

Beck, L., & Muia, J. A. (1980). A portrait of a tragedy: research findings on the dropout. *The High School Journal*, 64(2), 65–72.

Caplan, N., Choy, M. H., & Whitmore, J. K. (1991). *Children of the Boat: A Study of Educational Success*. Ann Arbor, MI: University of Michigan Press.

Kronik, R. F., Peterson, L., Morton, J., & Smith G. (1989). Dealing with dropouts: A review of the literature and preliminary findings. *Education*, Vol. 110, No. 1, pp. 123–129.

Labov, W. (1982). Competing value systems in the inner city schools. In P. Gilmore & A. Glatthorn (eds.), *Children In and Out of Schools*. Washington, D.C.: Center for Applied Linguistics, pp. 148–171.

Villegas, A.M. (1988). School failure and cultural mismatch: Another view. *The Urban Review*, Vol. 20, No. 4, pp. 243–265.

19. Hayes, C. (2012). Why elites fail. *The Nation*. June 6, 2012. *This article is adapted from* Twilight of the Elites: America After Meritocracy, *© 2012 by Christopher Hayes and published by Crown Publishers, a division of Random House Inc.*

20. Einstein, A. (1930). Religion and science. *New York Times Magazine*.

9

Freedom

4. **Freedom** (Choosing to engage or disengage with people in order to move into alignment with one's authentic self)

"A Blessing for Saying 'No'"
Blessed be the light that shines
in saying "no,"
the courage of self
singing its claim into the world.
Michael S. Glaser, *Disrupting Consensus*[1]

Entanglement and Freedom are two concepts intricately related. As seen in the first chapter, Entanglement refers to how we are influenced through attachments to social group identities and the roles that define the political and cultural dynamics of our schools and communities. Entanglement is driven by the human need for belonging and without awareness and attention to the undercurrents of this energy, it can impede agency for equity. Through the group dynamics of normative shared reality discourse, the innovation of new ideas is restricted. This often happens through a strict adherence to consensus building and various organizational devices that reward groupthink and reject critical thinking and creativity.

Einstein believed that "everything that the human race has done and thought is concerned with the satisfaction of deeply felt needs and the assuagement of pain. One has to keep that constantly in mind if one wishes to understand spiritual movements and their development." The assuagement of pain is the critical point behind the practice of Freedom. Freedom is the infinite potential found when moving out of constraining social dynamics that work to separate us from our Spirit Consciousness and end up draining our energy away from equity.

Freedom in Practice

A little more than a decade ago, when I was apprehensive about what was going on in the field of education, and as I began to formulate my ideas around Conscientious Engagement, I began an experiment in the practice of Freedom. I knew that I had to break out of old modes of thinking, disentangle myself from relationships that no longer served my life purpose and find a way to connect with others that had a similar life purpose. Towards this aim, I started *Real World Dialogue,* a platform and small creative publication for individuals who were interested in education for equity, diversity and community. For me, the idea of reaching out to people and engaging in dialogues and publishing them, like a journal, would capture organic snapshots of voice, which to me was a true experiment in agency. I hypothesized that if I invited strangers to discuss topics of equity, diversity and community in education, they would agree to engage with me in a dialogue that would reveal both in process and in purpose a new way of building community across social networks. The underlying premise of this exercise was through meaningful dialogue grounded in one's life purpose, people are willing to engage with people outside their traditional social circles and arrive at an expanded worldview. According to Freire, "Dialogue is an existential necessity. Dialogue is the encounter in which the united reflection and action of the dialoguers are addressed to the world which is to be transformed and humanized."[2]

I was able to solicit the participation of Dr. Xaé Alicia Reyes (Professor Emeritus of Education & Puerto Rican & Latino Studies at the University of Connecticut-Storrs) and Hector Luis Alamo, Jr. (Blogger and Associate Editor, @BeingLatino). When I originally reached out to Xaé and Hector via email, I was apprehensive. How might they respond? Would they be willing to engage? None of us knew each other. Xaé was still working at the University at the time. She has expertise in the areas of critical ethnography and teacher preparation for linguistically and culturally diverse communities. She is the author of the book, *How the Language and Culture of Scholars Affects Their Choice of Subjects and Methods of Research: Investigating the Researchers Habits of Mind*. Hector, at the time, was a young blogger whose work I discovered via social media. I was happy to discover my hypothesis was correct. They both agreed to engage and they both agreed to allow me to publish the results. I called it *Outsiders: Latino Perspectives on Voice, Agency and Leadership*. The topic was in response to my observation of the persistent portrayal of Latinos in media as cleaning ladies and gardeners. I wanted to know how these images influence Latino identity and even more importantly, how might these images impact our expectations of Latino youth in schools.

This dialogue demonstrated the potential of randomly connecting voices across fields, gender and age to discuss a topic that all three participants were invested in. Outside of the fact that we were all Latino, each of us moved in completely different circles. Several themes surfaced in the dialogue such as the wide range of characteristics that define the Latino community, which we acknowledged is extremely diverse. The topic of status attached to language, skin color or hair type came up. Latinos having to own up to feelings about class and poverty was discussed and we recognized how attachments to different social groups prevented Latinos from galvanizing around important issues that affect all Latinos, like the quality of schools. We discussed how teachers need to be aware of the nuances of identity that influence Latino children and how they need to understand that healthy social development is crucial to academic success.

> Teachers need to interact and collaborate with others who may not function within the same circles and traditionally established relationships but who share a similar life purpose and are committed to Conscientious Engagement.

Engaging in a public dialogue as a practice of Freedom encourages agency. Teachers need to interact and collaborate with others who may not function within the same circles and traditionally established relationships but who share a similar life purpose and are committed to Conscientious Engagement. The practice of Freedom suggests that courage, creativity and innovation can flourish in organic relationships that come together through Spirit Consciousness. It publicly demonstrates that we are all interconnected and belong to this shared experience of life that has great purpose and meaning. Belonging in this sense becomes less about group dynamics back at the school but a much larger belonging to a shared purpose. Freedom does not mean you have to abandon all of your previous relationships, but rather through awareness of their structure and function in your life, you can determine whether or not they serve human evolution and your life purpose. You may find that you may choose to disengage with some people in order to release blocked energy. Remember, energy is the primary source of agency. Energy is needed to confront complex situations that will move us towards equity. Although you may choose to disengage with some, you will discover that with the cleared space, you will begin to attract new people into your life who will support you and your work for equity.

My connection with Xaé evolved into a long-term professional relationship. After the article was published we continued communicating and years later, we met face to face. There are bodies of literature on teacher development, teacher retention and school change that are rife with accounts of collaborative efforts intended to ensure good teaching and the conditions that enable it. Most studies focus on supportive relationships of immediate colleagues. Few consider the supportive ties that extend to individuals beyond school walls and/or the education profession.[3] In her exploration of teachers' social networks within the context of the urban, high-needs schools as a manifestation of teacher agency, Anderson found that cultivating relationships outside one's immediate circles helps amass resources that increase capacity to enact change within the school context. Further, in proactively reaching out to individuals outside the school, teachers feel more effective and secure in their efforts to attain equity-minded goals.[4]

Trusting Authentic Relationships with Equity in Mind

On one occasion in my career, I had to rely on Xaé's support and guidance. She helped me feel more secure in my efforts to advocate for equity even at a time I felt my job was at risk. Here is an excerpt from our conversation that grew out of this conflict:

Raquel: *I'm wondering about how we can build trusting, authentic relationships in education. I see a lot of false generosity. "False generosity" is when a group of people who are historically seen as pedagogical authorities and hold leadership positions in the field say they want to transform the unjust order but because of their background they believe that they must be the executors of the transformation. They talk about the people, but they do not trust them; and trusting people is the indispensable precondition for revolutionary change.[5] When it comes to my work and my survival in advocating for equity, I think this is important to consider—How can we build and support authentic working relationships that extend outside our social identity groups for equity? In my experience, some groups, like Latino women, for example, are always seen as not having what it takes for leadership and they are treated with lesser value. Could it be because many historically marginalized groups have non-conventional, or "second tier" credentials or is it because of racism or both? Do credentials level the playing field?*

Xaé: *Trust is informed by experience, or perhaps it should be. Some of us are socialized to be trusting and after we experience professional disappointments, and even betrayal, we fall into a pattern my older son calls "Rinse and Repeat" whereby we knowingly (in spite of being warned by others) mentor and share our work selflessly with others,* *risking cooption and ultimately misrepresentation of our work as their own. Yet our hope that it is all for the greater good prevails and we move on and continue to trust.*

Early in my career I might have blindly trusted anyone who I perceived had higher pedagogical authority. Perhaps during my first iteration in graduate school I began to see dynamics of power relationships and inner circles that challenged my notions of pedagogical authority. Who had really earned it through his or her merits? Who had ascended to this role only through the legacy of relationships and networking? This skepticism did not take root because I distanced myself from academic circles for a number of years, so I continued to trust those holding pedagogical authority because I decided that what I had seen was limited to the one academic environment I was immersed in. I really believed other contexts would be different.

I worked in a variety of non-academic settings where political connections defined possibilities; the most dramatic was the appointment of a young woman to a technical, well-paying position only because she was in the fold of the political party where the top executive was engaged. She sat at her desk filing her nails and sitting pretty. I continued to see similar appointments over time and again when I returned to academic settings. My trust for those in leadership positions was somewhat fragile but a few random interactions with some faculty in leadership roles helped sustain it. When it began to wane, I made the decision to pursue a PhD because I attributed my vulnerabilities and proclivities to being used for my skills but not rewarded, or better yet being overlooked in favor of someone in the inner circle, as a consequence of my lack of credentials. I told myself this was the reason although I saw plenty of examples where the lack of credentials was not an obstacle.

Entering my doctoral program full of faith and trust in a new universe, I was led to my work in bilingual education and was exposed to presentations and writings of Henry Trueba and Kenji Hakuta. The program that funded me had leadership and some faculty that had similar backgrounds. I was ecstatic and pedagogical authority and trust rose. I was part of a cohort where a few of us were older and experienced in education but also in other fields, and I felt confident and excited. In a short time I uncovered other dynamics that I was unaccustomed to: intra- and interethnic conflict. I learned that I was part of the larger category of Latinos but not part of the predominant ethnic group in the region. Although I harmonized with everyone, I did note preferential treatment and support dispensed to the members of that ethnic group. Two female professors, in particular, although kind to me, were clearly partial and protective of students from their own group, to the point of grading inequitably and assigning superior grades for work not done or of inferior quality. These episodes and others began to erode my trust and respect for pedagogical authority once again. I was able to balance the negatives through meaningful interactions with a few other faculty members of the same background who were supportive and inclusive in their work with me. My survival and completion were in great measure due to my focusing on the experiences gleaned through positive interactions and validation of my work from a few folks with similar backgrounds and others with higher pedagogical authority who were mainstream but often guided by the more culturally informed colleagues.

I look at these two concepts (trust and value) and see a symbiotic relationship in my world. If I value you and find reciprocity in our mutual validation, trust emerges. This has often led me to confuse someone's need for my support and agency for true validation of my work and of who I am as a person and a professional. Unfortunately, all too often, a student has "acted" interested and committed to the issues I hold dear for the duration of the course and they completely disconnect once the grades are posted. Many times I am approached by a colleague who wants to "pick my brain" and this is followed by publications, grants, appointments and other rewards to this colleague and any prior connection to my "brain" is forgotten or ignored. One ends up learning a lesson but forgetting it all too quickly anytime someone else seeks our help and support because we are committed to a greater purpose of trying to improve educational opportunities for all.

Freire's notion of "false generosity" is powerful and I see it in our institutions at the national and state levels, and in our contexts. In a news piece I skimmed through recently, administrators discussed rewarding experiences and described assisting colleagues in leadership development as one of these. All of the participants mentioned were mainstream faculty and had been recommended by their mainstream department chairs. I finished reading in dismay over the lack of diversity and also felt a lack of validation of professional experiences people of different backgrounds could bring to the table. Maybe there is a very powerful notion that in the establishment, the legacy picks are the only *ones capable of transforming the hegemonic patterns their ideologies continue to reproduce, reminding me of Michael Apple's writings and Antonia Darder's work. There is such reluctance and resistance to shift the paradigm and allow other ideologies to permeate the educational agenda.*

This relates to the challenges of recruiting underrepresented individuals into teaching, yet any proposal coming from a person of an underrepresented background to remedy this seems to lack the pedagogical authority to be taken seriously and to influence policy in any consequential way. Ideas are lost and watered down due to the lack of cultural understanding and are led by folks who have not invested the time or have no history dealing with these issues. So our children have generationally failed to see themselves in the role of educators and educational leaders, and they are definitely not getting the modeling and information needed to effect change in the status quo.

My disappointments over these exclusionary practices have pushed me to engage in mentoring and outreach experiences to compensate for the lack of pedagogical authority I feel in my own academic roles. I reflect on the dynamics and find a way to subvert the order and engage in discourses of empowerment that may foster opportunities for other underrepresented individuals and encourage them to find a way to access the leadership roles wherever and whenever the opportunities present themselves, regardless of whether it means going through another institution. I think my upbringing was grounded in the mantra of "Querer es Poder" (where there's a will there's a way) and I often tell students and colleagues to persist and fight the system. My career path has been fraught with struggle and obstacles that I have witnessed being removed and smoothed out for others to place them in leadership roles and grant them promotions. Although I have been frustrated and at times disappointed I do not let anger or sadness over these practices prevail, I learn ways to help others and seek opportunities for professional gratification elsewhere.

Xaé, now retired, recently informed me that she now has more time to engage with several Church ministries such as food pantries and initiatives to further social justice. Equity education is an area she continues to prioritize in any teaching and consulting she takes on.

The Role of the Internet

Although the Internet has been a critical platform for me in my practice of Freedom, I do want to mention the limitations inherent in technology. Learning networks and online learning platforms do help educators expand their thinking by fostering relationships outside the school; however, you have to be wary of the power of information and reputation. Technology is often depicted as "decontextualized." It is imagined as having the power to communicate and convey information stripped of the encumbrances of social relationship, as well as the physical limitation of travel.[6] However, Frankham points out that knowledge construction within current learning networks can reproduce homogeneity and promote pedagogical authority for some by obscuring the inevitable power relations that exist.[7] Learning networks, according to Frankham, have arguably been hijacked by institutions and corporations that superimpose protocols, rules, procedures, structures and criteria for "success," that result in the mere reproduction of knowledge rather than true innovation. Nonetheless, electronic technologies and social media are the new tools for professional learning relationships. Due to advancements in technology people are experiencing Freedom by reaching out to people all across the globe rooted in mutual interests and the passion for social change. Through social media such as Twitter, LinkedIn and Facebook, teachers are interacting with others, sharing ideas and revealing information that is essential to our understanding of equity. We now get a glimpse at the world way beyond the four walls of a classroom. By exercising Freedom through the Internet, I have met people who have challenged my ideas, helped put my thinking into broader perspective and, more importantly, provided me with insight into patterns across contexts that give weight to emerging viewpoints.

Other Ways Teachers Practice Freedom

There are other perhaps more immediate and consequential ways that teachers can exercise the practice of Freedom that are important to include in this chapter. The practice of Freedom will often require a confrontation with people you work with who are conditioned by a shared normative reality that by way of your own individual Spirit Consciousness will appear not to be in the best service of equity. In other words, agency for equity is often operationalized through an individual's willingness to confront the forces of group dynamics. Steve McIntosh, author and President of the Institute for Cultural Evolution, points out that groups are intersubjective systems that are not self-aware like the individual, nor do they have a will of their own. Groups do not have the same moral value as an individual. Individuals are the bearers of evolution; they are the ones who ultimately make decisions and bear responsibility.[8]

> Agency for equity is often operationalized through an individual's willingness to confront the forces of group dynamics.

With this in mind, here is one more story on my practice of Freedom. When working as a teacher, I was faced with a dilemma. I became aware of child abuse. The child, who was part of my homeroom, had significant academic, social and emotional needs. He was constantly in trouble. He had difficulty engaging in most school activities and bounced around from classroom to classroom. He spent a great deal of time in the office. He was an African-American boy, large for his age with flailing arms, and the warmest eyes. He overwhelmed many of the teachers and students with his lack of boundaries. It was the behavior of a child that suffered from neglect, an unstable home environment and perhaps other influences of which I was not aware. In my observation, the school principal cared about his well-being to some extent. She allowed him great latitude. As a consequence, he often paraded about with little consequence to his actions. I did not personally observe any significant academic, social and emotional intervention on his behalf. Many of the students in my class suffered. They experienced fear and anxiety because on the bad days, this child became a bully and demanded all of my attention. The culture of the school was to accommodate, contain and redirect. The staff was unskilled and few teachers were learned in behavior modification practices and as far as I could tell, accountability measures and recordkeeping by the administration were negligible.

One day, this student came to school and could hardly walk or sit without wincing in pain. We went to the park that day and I watched him suffering. We sat on a bench and talked. I was able to get enough information to confirm my analysis of the situation. After conferring with my mother who is a social worker, I decided it was best to report the incident. When I did, I was reprimanded by the principal and then ostracized by many staff members in the school community. The principal told me that I had overreacted and that I was not familiar with the culture of the child's family. She said I should have consulted with her first. The truth is I knew she would have discouraged me from taking the situation to the authorities. Although I know that my reporting of the incident was the right thing to do, I had challenged the prevailing norms of the school. Later I realized that the norms were a form of protection. The administration did not want to call any attention to the school because they were in many ways out of compliance.

My challenge of the group norm in order to help this child who I had grown to care deeply about put my job and social standing in the school at risk. The last few weeks before leaving the school were difficult and strained. Many members of the school community stopped talking to me. My action caused discomfort and only now in retrospect do I realize that my actions most likely caused them to reflect on their own silence. Freedom means you have to have the courage to take a stand, or walk away from situations. This ruptures the bonds of comfortable relationships and may very well put your job security at risk.

Relationships are in your life for a purpose. Through our entanglements we are always faced with choices. Sometimes we are faced with the difficult decision to confront or leave a toxic relationship, school, organization, committee or other group configuration. Changing the dynamics of your relationships requires courage. Freedom is one of the most difficult practices of Conscientious Engagement because most of us are scared of being alone and petrified of the consequences that come with Freedom. Through history, we have witnessed the suffering that people endure when they act and fight for Freedom. However, the energy that we invest in relationships that no longer serve the dictates of Spirit Consciousness and equity do take a toll on our individual and collective social, emotional and spiritual well-being. In schools and organizations riddled with poor working conditions and questionable expectations and policies, the practice of Freedom may feel impossible. Few can withstand the pressure from groups, teams, committees and relationships that have some form of power over our destiny, whether it is socially or economically. It is not easy to advocate for the well-being of a child or a family that will put your own children and family at risk and yet—this is the heart of the matter. Freedom is an act of love. Trusting your Spirit Consciousness and exercising Freedom releases creative energy into the world, in ways that you cannot imagine. You will find that you are not alone and any suffering that you think you will experience as a result of your expression of Freedom is far lesser in degree than the suffering of silence and complicity.

Reflection Questions

1. What does it mean to be free of Entanglements? What would you do differently if you were a "free agent"?
2. Have you ever expressed thoughts to a group that disrupted consensus or challenged the status quo? What was that experience like? What was the result?
3. How might you channel energy in ways that will attract relationships into your life that will move you towards a greater commitment to equity?
4. How might you gently move away from relationships that are thwarting your Spirit Consciousness and your purpose to work for equity?

Notes

1. Glaser, M. S. (2009). *Disrupting Consensus*. Primedia E-launch LLC.
2. Freire, P. (1970). *Pedagogy of the Oppressed*. *30th Anniversary Reprint* (2003). New York: Continuum, pp. 88–89.

3. Anderson, L. (2010). Embedded, emboldened, and (net)working for change: Support seeking and teacher agency in high needs schools. *Harvard Educational Review*, Vol. 80, No. 4 p. 541.

4. Ibid.

5. Freire, P. (1970). *Pedagogy of the Oppressed. 30th Anniversary Reprint* (2003). New York: Continuum, pp. 94–95.

6. Strather, M. (2002). Abstraction and decontextualisation: An anthropological comment. In S. Woolgar (ed.), *Virtual Society? Technology, Cyberbole, Reality*. Oxford: Oxford University Press, pp. 302–313.

7. Frankham, J. (2006). Network utopias and alternative entanglements for educational research and practice. *Journal of Education Policy*, Vol. 21, No. 6, pp. 661–677.

8. McIntosh, S. (2007). *Integral Consciousness and the Future of Evolution: How the Integral Worldview is Transforming Politics, Culture and Spirituality*. St. Paul, MN: Paragon House, p. 27.

10

Meliorism

5. **Meliorism** (Through human effort we can imagine and build a better world)

"The goal is not to be better than the other man, but to be better than your previous self."

Dalai Lama[1]

Years ago I attended a Project Zero conference at Harvard where I had the pleasure of hearing David Perkins speak. He started his talk in such a clever way. When I walked into the large lecture hall, the first thing I noticed was the title of his PowerPoint presentation. In large bold type letters it read, *"Taming the wild and wilding the tame."* The slide showed a backdrop of a jungle followed by a perfectly manicured lawn, the kind you might see in front of one of those enormous homes in the Hamptons or Westchester County. With just a few choice words and two pictures, Perkins was able to capture the entire conundrum of education reform.

Education research and the large public–private partnership contracts that go along with it are ostensibly aimed at improving teaching and learning. However, when you look more closely, the education industry is more about how we transform, turn around, reform, and "tame" poor, at-risk students and struggling communities by way of the great American equalizer, education. The notion of *taming the wild* and the business that comes with it came into focus when I worked for a whole-school reform organization headquartered in Massachusetts. One day in particular comes to mind. It was the day we were told to buy large quantities of chocolate candy to distribute to the poor, brown children in one Boston school as compensation for several days of testing we were charged with administering. The test was a way to capture proof of the impact of our program, which as far as I was concerned was ambitious considering the many variables outside our control. My colleague and I spent a lunch hour venting and trying to make sense of our lives. We felt that our work was demeaning and dishonest.

There is countless research in education that results from experiments conducted in schools that serve poor students of color. It is not surprising then that much of public education discourse and funding is centered on how to get poor children of color to achieve academic success. Certainly, this must have something to do with the "taming of the wild" motif Perkins referred to that day at Harvard. It does so well at capturing the purpose of education. In the last decade, we have seen how this taming motif has now expanded to teachers. Education policy and practice operationalized through evaluations, standards-driven professional development and in-service training subjugates teachers to the same dominant narratives that have succeeded in drowning out the creative Spirit of teachers, which would otherwise ensure that teachers are in the right mind and position to protect the true democratic character of public education. Instead of taming, teaching and learning would be about loving children and encouraging the dispositions and skills they will need to address the urgent matters of our time, such as climate change and environmental

> Education policy and practice operationalized through evaluations, standards-driven professional development and in-service training subjugates teachers to the same dominant narratives that have succeeded in drowning out the creative Spirit of teachers.

catastrophe, income inequality and economic stability, fascism, xenophobia and nuclear war.

There was one other occasion that this phrase, the taming of the wild, came into clarity. It was when I was standing in line at an elaborate buffet in a hotel lobby during an education reform conference. A veteran in the field leaned over and hissed "poverty pimps" as she helped herself to a large serving of seafood pasta. This was several years ago and it was the first time I had heard this term, although I would hear it on many occasions afterwards.

In all fairness, Perkins was probably not intentionally referring to the big business of education reform or issues of equity when he used the term "taming the wild" in his presentation that day. Likewise, I do not consider all of education reform to be duplicitous. I am proud of the good work teacher educators do in service of supporting principals and teachers in schools, even in the poorest districts. We need "change agents" in education that are free to travel across the country. Change agency requires experience, a broad perspective and time to scour the best and most current research in order to come into a school with the level of energy and freshness needed to inspire teachers and administrators often mired down in the weeds. Project Zero and Perkins have been dedicating their research to arts in education for almost 50 years. When Perkins framed his talk around the phrase *taming the wild and wilding the tame*, what he was really doing was urging educators not to reduce teaching and learning to data-driven decision-making and to acknowledge our tendency to blindly focus on academics at the expense of creativity and imagination. Still, I like to think that there was something deeper, like a hidden clue in the matrix that asks, what does it mean for a teacher to be a change agent in an impoverished school district?

Visions of Equity

In his book *Teaching Toward Freedom*, Dr. William Ayers, Distinguished Professor at the University of Illinois at Chicago, argues that teaching at its best is an enterprise devoted to enlightenment and freedom, to the cause of humanity itself, and that teachers are often caught between that romantic-sounding ideal and the grubby business of domination and coercion that is the hallmark of so much that we call schooling.[2] Words like *enlightenment* and *freedom* resonate at very high levels when you meditate upon them. What does enlightenment and freedom look like, sound like, feel like in the school setting? How can we operationalize that? I'm especially curious when he says teachers *continuously get snarled in the web of domination and coercion.* How can we protect, develop and support teachers and school leaders in such a way that protects their creative spirit for equity in education? Meliorism is the belief that through human effort, we can better the world. If this is true, we need to ask, what is this better world we aspire to? What is the human effort required if we are to work towards this goal?

Ayers writes:

> *I would like to see all teacher-preparation and graduate programs offer a course study grounded in the humanistic mission of the enterprise: Turning toward the Student as a Fellow Creature; Building a Republic of Many Voices and a Community with and for Students; Feeling the Weight of the World through Your Own Lifting Arms; Teaching toward Freedom . . . I want teachers to figure out what they are teaching for and what they are teaching against. I want to teach against oppression and subjugation, for example, and against exploitation, unfairness, and unkindness, and I want others to join me in that commitment . . . I want teachers to commit to a path with a certain direction and rhythm: become a student of your students first, and then create a lively learning community through dialogue; love your neighbors; question everything; defend the downtrodden; challenge and nourish yourself and others; seek balance.[3]*

Ayers's vision presents us with some very important entry points as we consider what teaching and learning for equity looks like. However, I suspect that for meliorism to work, we cannot be handed a simple answer, rather we must engage in the self-examination and shared inquiry of reflecting on this question. The blind adoption of another man's words relinquishes our personal responsibility for the work at hand and gives ownership to another, outside ourselves. What does teaching and learning for equity in education look like, for *you*? How might a school or a school district function if building an egalitarian society were the primary purpose? When we reject the idea that adult learning and professional development can happen by borrowing and adopting the words from the outside world (great theorists, educators and politicians), we give credence to our own intelligence, our own capacity to make meaning and come to an understanding about important ideas that will steer the direction of our work and by extension, our world. This is not to say that we do not learn from wisdom. It just implies that we too are wise through the process of Conscientious Engagement. What type of *human effort* is required of us then?

Ayers recognized that teaching for humanization is hard, tough work, therefore it would seem it is more likely to be chosen by teachers who are wide awake to the true dimensions of the struggle.[4] I want to say Ayers is right, but I not sure anymore. Why? Let me tell you a story. A few years ago, I worked alongside a young, white, idealistic teacher assistant from a privileged background in a school that services all brown and black, mostly working class and poor students. She often picked my brain about the students as if I had some insight into their world. She observed me intently while I taught and praised my approach with them. She admitted on several occasions to the faults in her own communication and she was aware in some regard that her approach was not working. When we spoke, she shared anecdotes that she believed indicated racial tensions and misunderstandings. She told me she studied social justice pedagogy. One day, when she was frustrated, I offered her two books on white privilege. I think I gave her *Breaking the Code of Good Intentions* by Melanie Bush and the other, I don't recall, but it could have been one of Francis Kendall's books. I was hopeful that she would find these books useful. Three weeks later, she returned the books unread. She apologized that with her workload, she had no time to read them. I could not help wonder, how awake could this teacher be to the true dimensions of the struggle of oppression?

As we learned in previous chapters, teachers do enter the practice for altruistic reasons, yet it is important to examine this notion of altruism in a country where the vast majority of teachers are white women and the schools and communities in which they teach are segregated by race and class. Does meliorism translate within this context into the charity of "helping poor brown and black children succeed in society?" Meliorism, depending on the process by which we define a better world and channel our effort, can have powerful implications. The teacher as "missionary" is not a new concept.

Ansari writes in her dissertation:[5]

> *In the global context of Western imperialism and colonization, missionaries have historically occupied a very complicated space with respect to the "natives" they hoped to help, transform, shape, enlighten and so forth. While missionaries may have participated individually to "ameliorate" the lives of native peoples through their work of education, this work was also complicit with motive of political and economic expansion on behalf of the institutions they served and represented (Achebe, 1989; Bhabha, 1990, 1994; Hitchens, 1995; Saidd, 1994a; 1994b; Spivak, 1987, 1994, 1999; Tiberondwa, 1980). Analogously, the work of missionaries in educating freed slaves in the South during the post-Civil War Reconstruction period was equally fraught with complications. Williams (2005) explored the subjectivity of missionary teachers and the paternalistic ways in which their work was framed by historians, noting specifically how freed people were broadly regarded not as participants, but rather as subjects. The language of uplift, revitalization, and saving is a broad conceptualization that many missionaries had about their work in the South, and how that work was practiced. Analogously, urban spaces are also more broadly conceptualized in both culture and educational discourse as spaces that need civilizing.*

If teachers weren't altruistic and meliorists, we'd probably have a much greater teacher shortage than we currently have in some states. However, considering the demographics and historical implications of our work in education, it might be useful for us to question how a disposition of altruism might benefit our work for equity and how it might create barriers to building an egalitarian society. Altruism is a *selfless* concern for the well-being of another. It can foster the "teacher as hero" archetype or as stated earlier, teacher as "missionary," in which case teachers act as mediators between their students' academic success and future self-actualization, which Ansari argues enacts a power dynamic in which educators are always the key drivers of change.[6] What type of inner and outer work do teachers need to do if they are aware of these power dynamics that are often perpetuated within racially segregated school communities and society?

Good Intentions Gone Wrong

Here is a situation that reveals the complexity of our good intentions. I was in attendance at an education conference when a white presenter with a doctorate in education and leadership position at a prestigious university shared a story. I will call her Jane. Jane shared how her black colleague struggled with a public presentation that she was preparing. According to Jane, every time her black associate rehearsed her presentation in front of colleagues, the feedback was that she was too emotional and it took away from the message. Jane shared how terrible she felt. She believed the situation had everything to do with race. She told us that if she offered to deliver the presentation for her colleague, as a white woman, it would most likely appeal to a broader audience, folks who really needed to hear her important research.

This situation is a perfect example of how confusing it can be for even very highly educated people to determine what kind of human effort is required if we are to work for equity. It demonstrates how good intentions of individuals often perpetuate inequitable power relationships. How does it help our work in building an egalitarian society if a white woman delivers the research presentation designed by a black woman when there is a dearth of black and Latino educators with the authority and platform to reach the public? I also suspect that Jane was convinced that her storytelling revealed an injustice in the world *out there*, rather than revealing contradictions within her own line of thinking.

Recently, I came across a hashtag on Twitter circulating called #WhiteLiberalProverbs. One image that speaks to this point depicts a white woman who has one hand draped over her chest and the other hand covering the mouth of a brown woman who looks frustrated. While the brown woman's eyes are wide open, the white woman's eyes are closed but her mouth is agape as she cries, "You poor ignorant stupid fool who has internalized racism! Don't worry, I'll fight the good fight for you since you are obviously too brainwashed to know better. I'll be offended on your behalf!" The comic can be found here: http://www.memes.com/img/650585

Often an altruistic stance, or a good intention, results in misdirected energy that may advocate a message but does not translate to the type of work needed to right inequitable conditions and relationships. This is because we do not engage in the process of self-examination and the examination of our structures and processes that perpetuate racist, hegemonic ideologies in spite of our good intentions. In this last example, Jane reveals through her storytelling the focus of her work, which is on the message. She said, "her powerful words should really get out there and reach a wider [white] audience." This does not address the racism that is reinforced by whites who are often in positions of authority and privilege feeling the need to speak for black folks, while they remain backstage regardless of their hard work or intellectual capacity. Furthermore, there was no mention of the role she plays in this dynamic, nor of her colleagues providing feedback about the style of presentation that is laden with racial implications. Rozena Maart, black South African philosopher, does a very good job explaining this in her article "Race and Pedagogical Practices: When Race Takes Center Stage in

Philosophy." In it she draws attention to the ways in which black presence, in the flesh—as teacher, professor, researcher, scholar—when accounted for within empirical research[7,8] is either treated with suspicion or seen as *too much*.[9] How can we work with Jane to be more aware of her own role within the socio-political, socio-cultural dynamics of racism? How can we build knowledge around the types of everyday practices that transform our good intentions into behaviors that can really make a difference in our work for equity?

False Generosity and Obstructions to Our Realization of Equity

According to John Dewey, meliorism is the belief that the specific conditions which exist at one moment, be they comparatively bad or comparatively good, in any event may be bettered. He states meliorism encourages intelligence to study the positive means of good and the obstructions to their realization, and to put forth endeavor for the improvement of conditions.[10] Meliorism is a positive thing and necessary for our work for equity. It is akin to hope. The emphasis is that meliorism encourages *intelligence to study the positive means of good and the obstructions to their realization*. This is critical because it addresses how we can ensure that we don't fall into pseudo-meliorism or what Freire called, "false generosity." In other words, it helps us to identify the practice.

The proper use of our intelligence towards the study of good and bad and obstructions to our realization happens when we stop all efforts to fix things and retreat into a period of mindful inquiry. This is thoughtful deliberation, non-judgmental observation and dialogue. Only in this way can we can find the clarity and heightened awareness needed to get past the clutter of our words, the labels we attached to our perceptions of reality and other illusions that without consciousness, easily translate into actions that may in fact work against our goals for equity. Educators are particularly susceptible to misguided actions because we often narrow the focus of our work to serve the intellect. It is only through stillness, retreat, non-judgmental observation and dialogue that we can enrich the Spirit, which is the gateway to Consciousness. Consciousness illuminates the space where thought and action meet.

Have we really taken the time to confront our failure to realize social justice and equity? Have we examined how it is that we have elected someone like Trump into presidential office, a man who built his campaign on fear, hate and xenophobia? Is this who we are? Is this what we have become? The illusion of a democracy, the illusion of equity, the illusion that we respect and honor the diversity in our country has been perfectly designed and organized in our minds. You can see how this illusion has manifested in society. If you were to conduct a quick search on the Internet around the terms "equity in education" and "social justice" I guarantee you will find hundreds of organizations, committees and advocacy groups out there, all of them fighting for justice and equity. Why is it then that if we are investing such an inordinate amount of human effort into this work, we are living a time in history with alarming levels of income disparity, domestic and international terrorism based on race and religion, and a school system that is segregated in spite of the decision in *Brown vs. Board of Education* in 1954?

Are we perhaps ensnarled in the illusion of our false words and actions that do nothing to indicate we have a real belief and commitment to equity? Are we perhaps implicated in this business of breaking things and fixing things and creating suffering so that we can be heroes? Is it possible that we have lost our moral compass and have been left fragmented and frustrated by the emptiness of so much *superficial activity* that has become a lively diversion for academics and donor elites? What would be revealed by *removing things* that stand in the way of our realization of equity, to engage in the real art of living, not unlike sculpture, in which the artist creates, not by building, but by hacking away?[11]

A young, white, female millennial walks into a school in the poorest section of the Bronx; she has been given the authority and a meager salary to lead a social justice effort. We cannot mistake this situation as being an authentic act of agency for equity. Why? Because why is this woman leading this endeavor really, in this context and at this time and with a salary in the midst of abject poverty? For whom is she speaking? Was there no one in the community who was able to perform this role? Has she done the inner and outer work required? How do we know? When she opens her mouth to speak, she starts by apologizing for her white privilege (which is what the Managing Director of Unbound Education did in her opening remarks at the Standards Institute in Washington). Still, this situation that we see every day is tiring and offensive because the question remains the same. Was there no one from the community who could perform this task?

Over the course of my career in education, I have witnessed many good-intentioned white educators in positions of leadership who manage and lead people of color (and/or people with a heritage of poverty) who have a wealth of knowledge, intellectual capacity and leadership ability but who are never recognized, developed or acknowledged for their true worth. Often, these passed-over individuals have credentials that go systematically ignored or undervalued. I have also witnessed good-intentioned leaders cry real tears in the professional space when they are horrified by an event like the death of Eric Garner that reveals persisting racial inequality and injustice, or the inhuman and brutal treatment of the water protectors in North Dakota— yet they are in front of a black or brown subordinate listening sympathetically, who wouldn't dare cry on the job, even though they worry that their black husband might be shot coming home at night. How is it possible to build an equitable, human society while keeping the same members of the oppressor group in all the positions of authority? It is simply not possible. For alternative modes of social interaction and the transformation of our society to an egalitarian one, members of the oppressed groups themselves, those that have been victimized and abused by racism, inequitable policies and practice and who by no fault of their own continue to struggle to reclaim their voice and understand freedom, *must be at the center of the movement*. This does not mean that people from privilege or whiteness should disappear or not participate in the process. Political power is essential to the process and so we must learn to work in partnership, but a partnership for equity does require we remove historically privileged groups from the center of change.

Meliorism implies *collective effort*. That is, not "I" action but rather "We" action. Within all collective action, there is the consideration of those who have been denied their primordial right to speak their word and who must first reclaim this right to prevent the continuation of this dehumanizing aggression.[12] We cannot expect positive results from any educational or political action program for equity that fails to respect the particular view of the world held by the people.[13] When we take the time to engage in deep reflection exercises through conscientious dialogue about what it means when we say "*we want a better world*" as well as what it means when we say "*collective effort*," then we will begin to understand not only where we are going, but how we need to reposition ourselves to get there.

> When we take the time to engage in deep reflection exercises through conscientious dialogue about what it means when we say "*we want a better world*" as well as what it means when we say "*collective effort*," then we will begin to understand not only where we are going, but how we need to reposition ourselves to get there.

As we begin to understand the great potential and danger of a melioristic stance, we need to pay special attention to the nature of our actions. If action is produced in name of *bettering the world*, but the action is emphasized exclusively, to the detriment of reflection (process), agency for equity is converted to mere *activism*, which is simply action for action's sake—which negates the true praxis,[14] thereby making Conscientious Engagement impossible. Through Conscientious Engagement we can critically analyze our good intentions and begin to determine how our behaviors in society operationalize these values, these ideals in such a way that disrupts inequality and inequitable social arrangements. It is the willingness to retreat and inquire in the true service of altruism through education, to see clearly the systemic and structural conditions that exist that prevent us from the realization of a better the world.

Reflection Questions

1. What is your vision of a better world? Why do you think we have not yet realized a vision for equity in education?
2. How does the current socio-cultural and political climate heighten your awareness around the challenges we face in education? Do you think the education community is implicated in the widening of inequality and the rise in xenophobia and/or fascist ideologies that now get so much attention in mainstream American media and politics?
3. What patterns have you noticed in education that may help to explain the disconnect between our passion for equity and our everyday practice?
4. How can you begin to heighten your awareness of the dynamics of power, race and class in your school, district and community?

Notes

1. For more information about the source of the Dalai Lama quote, read Dalai Lama, XIV. https://www.goodreads.com/author/quotes/570218.Dalai_Lama_XIV?page=4
2. Ayers, W. (2004). *Teaching Toward Freedom*. Boston: Beacon Press, p. 138.
3. Ibid., p. 18.
4. Ibid., p. 138.
5. Ansari, S. (2013). Deconstructing College-Readiness in an Urban Black Context: Ideology, Discourse, and Practices. Thesis. University of Illinois at Chicago. Achebe, C. (1989). *Hopes and Impediments: Selected Essays*. New York, NY: Doubleday. Bhabha, H. K. (1990). *Nation and Narration*. London, UK; New York, NY: Routledge. Bhabha, H. K. (1994). *The Location of Culture*. London, UK; New York, NY: Routledge. Hitchens, C. (1995). *The Missionary Position: Mother Teresa in Theory and Practice*. New York, NY: Verso. Said, E. W. (1994a). *Culture and Imperialism*. New York, NY: Vintage Books. Said, E.W. (1994b).

Orientalism. New York, NY: Vintage Books. Spivak, G. C. (1994). Can the subaltern speak? In P. J. Williams & L. Chrisman, *Colonial Discourse and Post-Colonial Theory: A Reader*. New York: Columbia University Press, pp. pp. 66–111. Spivak, G. C. (1999). Translation as culture. In I. C. Suárez, A. G. Fernández, & M. S. S. Lafuente (eds.), *Translating Cultures*. Hebden Bridge, UK: Dangaroo Press, pp. 17–30. Tiberondwa, A. K. (1980). *Missionary Teachers as Agents of Colonialism: A Study of Their Activities in Uganda, 1877-1925*. Kampala, UG: Fountain Publishers. Williams, H. (2005). *Self-Taught: African American Education in Slavery and Freedom.* Durham, NC: University of North Carolina Press.

6. Ansari, S. (2013). Deconstructing College-Readiness in an Urban Black Context: Ideology, Discourse, and Practices. Thesis. University of Illinois at Chicago.

7. hooks, b. (1994). *Teaching to Transgress: Education as the Practice of Freedom*. New York: Routledge.

8. Curry, B.R. (2004). Whiteness and feminism: Deja vu discourses, what's next? In G. Yancy (ed.), *What White Looks Like: African-American Philosophers on the Whiteness Question*. New York: Routledge.

9. Maart, R. (2014) Race and pedagogical practices: When race takes center stage in philosophy. *Hypatia*, Vol. 29, No. 1, pp. 205–220.

10. Dewey, J. (1920). *Reconstruction in Philosophy*. New York: Henry Holt and Company, p. 178.

11. Watts, A. (1951). *The Wisdom of Insecurity*. New York: Vintage Books.

12. Freire, P. (1970). *Pedagogy of the Oppressed. 30th Anniversary Edition* (2003). New York: Continuum, p. 88.

13. Ibid, p. 95.

14. Ibid.

11

Emergence

1. **Emergence** (Channeling human energy in ways that enable the integration of new ideas for equity)

"One needs a great deal of energy, vitality, interest to bring about a radical change in oneself. If we are interested in outward phenomena, we have to see what we can do with the rest of the world in the process of changing ourselves; and also we must see not only how to conserve energy, but how to increase it. We dissipate energy endlessly by useless talk . . ."
J. Krishnamurti,, *The Awakening of Intelligence*, 1973

A number of years ago I hit a brick wall in my career. I was desperately trying to find a job. I continued sending out resumes like a mad woman and interviewing for positions thinking that the more effort I put in, the more likely I was to land a job that matched my experience and qualifications. But no matter how much I pushed, no matter how much I lowered my expectations for salary, type of position or distance traveling, nothing happened. I couldn't understand why my efforts did not result in any change in my circumstances. In a short time, I became bitter and declared life unfair. I fell into a deep state of cynicism. This cynicism mixed with economic insecurity exhausted me to the point that even after a long sleep, I was lethargic and unmotivated in the morning. The letters I wrote to potential employers were now spotted with errors in spelling. My husband told me to stop trying so hard and to let go. These were difficult words to hear, and even harder to apply to my situation. How could I stop exerting effort at a time of such great urgency?

After a forced retreat in which I recharged my batteries, I got back to my desk. This time, I began to look at jobs that I had previously dismissed. I expanded my search to include jobs that spoke to my desire for adventure, change and creativity. These were all things that surfaced as being important during my retreat. That's when the unexpected presented itself. I came across an advertisement for a professional development specialist position in Abu Dhabi, the capital and second largest city in United Arab Emirates. The job sounded so amazing that the fact that I would have to leave my family felt like a trivial detail. I applied and got called rather quickly. I learned that this team would be responsible for designing and delivering training to over 600 principals, vice principals and faculty heads employed in the public schools in the United Arab Emirates. The UAE had just embarked on their first year of a ten-year reform initiative that would implement a student-centered, English–Arabic bilingual model in their public schools. They were rapidly employing English-speaking western teachers to work alongside Arab nationals in co-teaching teams and contracted an American company to help them manage this enormous undertaking. Within three weeks, I was on a plane to Abu Dhabi. Little did I know that this experience would not only change my life but it would help me to develop and practice the last principle of my theory, called Emergence, which is how we channel human energy in ways that enhance the integration of new ideas and the creation of an egalitarian society.

Every morning living in the UAE, I woke up to a beautiful prayer song resonating from the mosque. This would be the first time in my life I'd be surrounded by a whole community that put morning prayer, God and faith at the center of all things. With the ongoing bashing of the Arabic culture and Islam back home, I felt a little apprehensive about living in a Muslim country where women are not treated as equals. However, in a short time I began to feel at ease. I was grateful for the opportunity to learn and expand my understanding, which helped me to suspend judgment. At the leadership training, females wore the traditional Emirate clothing called the abaya. Some wore hijabs or fully covered their faces with a burqa. Women sat apart from the statuesque males dressed in bleached white kanduras, often accompanied by a gutrah headscarf. I found the female Emirate school leaders to be strong, caring and beautiful. They rarely shied away from saying what needed to be said. Sometimes the men in the room didn't turn or listen as intently as we would have liked, but to be fair, this does happen in the States, although we do not attach these occurrences to gender roles. Several of the women were outspoken and exhibited a unique kind of agency that appeared to be perfectly in sync with the nuances of their culture and context. Being in their presence enhanced my understanding of teacher agency for equity because it surfaced issues related to the role of culture, language and gender. As I said, my stay in the Middle East became an experiment in the practice of Emergence. I was mindful of how I could channel my energy in ways that enabled the integration of new ideas for equity.

One revealing incident occurred at a school leadership training session in Abu Dhabi. We asked a room full of female Emirate principals to identify one individual in their school building that could be relied on to help them lead the transformation effort. They were to write down the individual's name and reflect on the characteristics that led them to choose this person. After providing the instructions, several principals called the interpreter over and asked her to clarify. Then, several more raised their hands and asked for clarification. As I watched the interpreter go around the room answering questions, women across the room started fidgeting, and murmuring to each other. I approached the interpreter and asked, "What is going on?" She was equally confused. She told me that she had explained the prompt in a variety of different ways and that the problem was not language. After several more minutes, one principal raised her hand and called me over to her table. She asked politely, "What is the purpose of this activity?" With the help of my interpreter I did my best to explain that part of understanding change leadership is knowing one leader can't do the work alone and that a good leader begins to identify talent amongst the staff to encourage shared leadership. She listened graciously and then told me she could not complete the exercise because it did not make sense. She explained that Emirate leaders have complete confidence in the talents of every member of their staff and that each person in the school would be equally responsible for leading the transformation. She finished by asking, "How is it possible to choose just one when I can trust and depend on everybody?"

I had to pause and then I realized that our individualist culture and worldview was driving how we designed our training and activities. As the Emirate principal rightly pointed out, the activity contained an embedded assumption about the nature of leadership and loyalty. In fact, many leadership training courses are based on the naïve assumption that one can promote community by training its leaders—as if it were the parts that promote the whole and not the whole which, in being promoted, promotes the parts.[1] For the principals to complete the task they would have had to reorient their thinking and deep-rooted notions of leadership and change movements. Change leadership from our point of view starts by focusing on empowering individual leaders who have some unique skill or disposition that can galvanize followers. Following the prompt and adopting our "theory of action" would imply a certain cultural invasion. Furthermore, a principal in that context would not feel comfortable identifying one individual in a public forum. That would be saying that the other workers in her school have "lesser value," which could backfire in many ways. This principal's willingness to raise her hand and inquire into the purpose of the activity, and then politely reject it by pointing out the hidden assumptions, was a brilliant act of agency for equity.

Channeling and Conserving Energy Effectively

Emergence is the *practice* of channeling our energy in ways that enable us to integrate new ideas for equity. Sometimes, the best way of channeling energy is to move into inaction, stillness, deliberation and inquiry. Often times, we don't stop and make room for questioning that helps us get past the surface to uncover normative shared realities that may not serve our primary purpose of equity, which implies the full integration of new ideas that come from diverse perspectives. How often are we given time in professional development to inquire into the purpose of the task, and its relevance and value to our work for equity? Often, pausing to reflect and inquire into a situation, taking the time to clarify meaning and purpose, regardless of the time it takes, provides us with critical insight into the nature of language, the nature of our normative shared reality and the nature of power relationships that may be driving the conversation. We are always in a rush with an agenda and a timetable that often works against integrity. Agency can be operationalized through a clear expectation that we have to slow down and allow all participants to critically examine the process before taking action. We don't want to drain our energy by engaging in behaviors that do not align with our purpose. When a participant in a training challenges the premise or the unchecked assumptions of the teacher, or "pedagogical authority," in the room, new possibilities arise to (re)valuate whether diverse and alternative points of view are taken into consideration.

Working and living in the UAE was the perfect opportunity for me to channel my energy differently. I was alone without my family, in a new space, in a completely new country. I had reached an impasse in my career so it was an ideal time to do this work. In this space, I was afforded the opportunity to check my assumptions on a daily basis about gender, culture, language and agency in education. I was able to heighten my awareness of the multilayered, political dynamics that impact our professional decisions inside and outside the school community. I was in the UAE at a very interesting time in history. They had been riding the wave of their acquisition of oil money which had changed the landscape at such rapid speed that young Emirates and expats alike forgot that it was only 60 years ago that Abu Dhabi was poor and suffered in the desert. Just a bit over one generation ago, the majority of the people were illiterate and members of a British colony. Rapid wealth forced the Sheiks to play catch-up with modern civilized countries in many areas, including building an infrastructure, developing business and updating the education system. Unfortunately, the Sheiks often turned to the same capitalists who were in the position to exploit Arab inexperience. Arab leaders prioritized the need for knowledge. This was good, but they needed it fast so that they wouldn't have to be dependent on outside experts and consultants. From the outside, Abu Dhabi appeared to be a modern-day ostentatious city with state-of-the-art technology, however on the inside they were young and new at cosmopolitan society. There were many tensions in this dynamic that affected our work there. Abu Dhabi fell into the center of a vicious vortex as western countries led by massive corporations vied for access to large profitable contracts to service their needs, contracts that included education and training.

As I got deeper into the work of designing and delivering leadership training for audiences that included both Emirate and English-speaking educators, I began to feel uneasy about our role there. This uneasiness stemmed from my growing awareness of the political context. There was concern and disagreement about how to manage change. For example, the English-speaking teachers did not understand Arabic nor did they understand the culture of the children. In the first year, the bilingual, student-centered model was launched in early elementary with the intention that each year it would move up a grade. In early elementary, children are for the first time leaving their homes so socialization, language and parent involvement are extremely critical to creating a positive teaching and learning environment. Emirate teachers were teamed with westerners to teach and lead the initiative but western teachers had questionable skills in teaching. It was difficult to recruit high-quality teachers from abroad expecting them to leave their countries behind and live in the Middle East. Regardless of experience, English-speaking teachers were given licenses to teach, often displacing nationals because licensure prioritized English fluency. This policy created strife in the communities where women looked to teaching jobs to stay involved in the rearing and education of children. English-speaking expats had difficulty communicating with children and parents so co-teaching arrangements were often strained. Numerous discussions in the training pointed to this frustration, greatly impacting the school climate. There was an overwhelming sense of confusion and powerlessness amongst the Emirate school leaders because the reform initiative came down from the top as a directive and they duly recognized the value of Arabic–English bilingualism and student-centered learning. Another contentious component of the New School Model was school hours were lengthened to build in more time for professional development. In theory, this makes perfect sense considering the work and learning involved in transformation; however, extending the hours of the workday had serious implications for the Emirates who had children and families to care for while having no impact whatsoever on the young, foreign teachers who were living in the Middle East alone.

What Does It Mean to Be at the Center of Transformation?

Over time, I became more and more sensitive to these tensions. To make matters worse, I often had to spend time in the district office where I observed leadership positions held by westerners. I was again at the center of a transformation with all of its peculiarities and again part of a team that had received a large sum of money to lead the work. No one would argue that the UAE can benefit from learning alternative approaches to designing learning environments for more a more student-centered education experience; however, was it possible that our role in the process was both unfair and indispensible? How could we help the Emirate community build more progressive schools without devaluing their native language and invading their culture? Patricia Ryan, an expat educator in the Middle East who delivered a wonderfully entertaining TEDex presentation, spoke at length about the dangers of the proliferation of English as a medium of instruction as a way to modernize schools and become competitive in the global economy. She points out how this same situation has been occurring in countries like Japan and all over the African continent. Often, transformation is spearheaded and managed by private companies, many of them American.

When I arrived back to the States, it took some time to synthesize my learning and figure out what I was supposed to do with it. In the practice of Emergence, we channel our energy in ways that enable us to integrate new ideas and further our work for equity. I decided to reach out to Carla, one of our interpreters. As a writer and a strong believer in the power of public dialogue, I suggested we collaborate together so that we could share our experience with others.

Carla Abdel Karim was born in Lebanon and had been living in Abu Dhabi for more than 29 years. She has a Master's and a teaching degree in translation and languages from St. Joseph's University in Lebanon. Currently, she is a writer at *The National* newspaper in Abu Dhabi. As I mentioned earlier, simultaneous interpreters, like Carla, were an integral part of our presentation team. They are the ones who translate everything we say into Arabic. They also follow presenters around the large rooms in order to translate group discussions. Carla and I worked effortlessly together. Over time we engaged in deep conversations about our perceptions of the cross-cultural communication taking place.

In the following excerpt, Carla discusses how language and culture influence our work as change agents, especially when change agents come from outside the native culture, creating real tensions:

Carla: You cannot impose a certain view or a certain mentality on people. In the UAE there is a completely different approach, a different perception, a different kind of vision for that matter, and you can't assume people will understand. You have to localize the vision to help people grasp the ideas. To be an agent of change, you need to research the culture and look into the language of the people. Language and culture go hand in hand. How does the language depict some notions . . . ? What does the terminology really mean? Terminology does not refer to the same concept when it is translated literally. There is a whole cultural luggage behind each word. What I mean is the upbringing, the religious principals, traditions, for example—there are words we cannot utter in Arabic because it would be a taboo, or it would bring about a topic that should not be mentioned in public. The trainees understand the concepts, but their understanding of it is quite cultural because the concepts need to be further elaborated.

One problem is the Arabic language is not prepped with the appropriate education terminology and research in this field does not yet exist in Arabic. It's just starting up, actually. The educational systems in other countries have been developed, whereas here it's a young nation in some respects. In the Arab world, education research has never been done in Arabic. Fields like law and medicine, these overlap, yes, but for education and pedagogy, these concepts have just recently started to exist and explored over the last two decades. We can take a few examples we've witnessed up front. We speak of the "Pedagogy Matrix" and "Smart Goals" in the trainings. These concepts are obvious for the trainer who has familiar notions, but translating these expressions without prior explanation makes no sense to those receiving the information in the frame of a consecutive interpretation. The word and the meaning, together, do not exist—nor are they meaningful in the target language. There's a term called terminological morpheme—which refers to the written form of the word. Each morpheme has a meaning or content behind it. This is the semantics of a language. Semantics is directly linked to the culture and language as it carries a lot of cognitive content—what a person has acquired and gathered over a lifetime. Using one term can bring in a total recall of how a person views or perceives the world. So, using terms from the source language for a people requires extensive explanation in the target language so they can grasp it within the frame of a verbal communication brought about by consecutive interpretation.

Another example of this would be the expression, "think outside the box." When we used that during training, we knew this was an untranslatable expression. We cannot tell someone in Arabic, think outside the box. You have to say, "be creative," for example. Yet, we don't want to simplify that term either but we have to do our best to use phrases to capture what is meant. Finding an exact equivalent is not always obvious in a given situation when you have to also be politically correct and appropriate for the context.

The language barrier was a tough one to cross. There is understanding when there is a dialogue that starts a real discovery of the appropriate terminology . . . that can only come from this live exchange. By building terminology in a specific language, you start building meaning and only then can these concepts be clarified before real teaching and learning starts. In the trainings that I have been a part of, sufficient time is usually not built in. Why? Because we want change to be immediate.

There is not enough interaction and we know that any teaching and learning operation has to include back and forth interaction to ensure that people are completely involved and they feel involved. They have to feel that they are part of this process. It is my understanding that leaders want change to happen quickly because there is a sense of urgency in matters of education. In order to compete with the rest of the region and the world, they need to build up future generations and the education infrastructure accordingly with the development of the country and the needs of a knowledge-based economy. You also have to prepare the community and society to be ready for this future. You need to raise awareness, while the process of reform is ongoing; you have to raise awareness not only through schools, but generally across the population. We should rely on schools to communicate this vision but we have to partner with different entities and organizations that work with the community.

There is urgency because at this time, the UAE is still a country riddled with consultants. They have had to rely on consultants because they come with experiences that are relevant and see best practice in the education field. But the Emirati are their own people, with valuable experiences as well. Why should anyone want to depend on consultants all the time? And that is why there is pressure for change . . . fast change in education. There are some consultancy firms hired for strategy planning, for example, but some are setting up strategies and systems that are not quite sustainable or readily implementable because they don't apply to the cultural or national context. This is a real challenge. We need to customize and prepare the ground, make sure the people understand the vision. When I work as an interpreter with educators, I can see that in discussions with them. I believe they can tell us if the vision is doable and whether or not it is achievable.

The Arab perception of knowledge is such that . . . Well, look, we have the greatest researchers . . . mathematicians—scholars such as Muḥammad ibn Mūsā al-Khwārizmī and Ibn Sīnā who did research in math and science, etc. Amazing discoveries . . . these are the people behind knowledge and were at one time translated to inform western knowledge and the great majority of western work is based on these ancient writings and scholars. Arabs were considered the holders of knowledge for centuries, at least until the beginning of the Renaissance. But then politics and globalization happened. When you start thinking about borders, wars, money, defending differences, you lose the sense of intellect and knowledge. Anything besides strategy and business becomes invalid throughout the world. The Arab world is rich in culture . . . but the problem is there was a breaking point and we have drifted. Now we depend on others to bring us an understanding of what education should look like.

The UAE is seeking to diversify its economy and wishes to do so by seeking best practices and experts across continents. Its people, its culture and its heritage are at the heart of the changes taking place. In this era of mass media and globalization, they have welcomed many different nationalities and cultures, and have above all, preserved their own. These practices are embedded in the Arab culture, the principals and vice principals need only to reposition themselves to identify and actuate them. How many times have we heard them say, "we know this" or "we already apply that?" They are referring to practices that already exist but have not been conceptualized or articulated in the same way. My message to them is always—we are not learning something new, merely returning to the greatness of our ancestors.

Implications of Language and Culture on Agency for Equity

Working in the Middle East and taking the stance of a Mindful Scholar practitioner through dialogue (in this case much like an ethnographer), we were able to identify major themes that could be applied to our work on building agency for equity. Carla highlighted many of these insights in our discussion:

◆ A vision and purpose must be customized, localized and put into the hands of the people themselves.
◆ Language and culture are interdependent, which requires built-in time for all participants to clarify terminologies and build meaning around new concepts.
◆ Transformation requires awareness, not just amongst a few in education but across the general population and through partnerships.
◆ Knowledge and best practices already reside within the culture, language and heritage of all people and therefore, education becomes about articulating, identifying and actualizing.

Putting the vision and purpose in the hands of the people themselves is critical. This includes poor people, who are often perceived as not having the skills, knowledge and dispositions to take equal part in the design and implementation of a progressive education vision. Dr. Frank Bonilla, an educator and scholar who founded the Center for Puerto Rican Studies at Hunter College, wrote in 1964:

> It is also vital and legitimate to fight poverty not only by spending public funds on the poor but by dedicating part of such funds to work among the non-poor employers, landlords, educators, government officials, politicians, labor leaders, and others whom the poor accept as leaders. Because the poor have the capacity to help themselves through the exercise of organizational, political, and social skills, they are to be mobilized and actively incorporated into the planning and execution of programs for self-help.[2]

Removing Ourselves from the Center

When we consider the practice of Emergence, we must understand that channeling energy with equity in mind is often removing ourselves from the center of action. This disrupts the power structure by allowing all participants to construct knowledge and meaning, which will inevitably result in the emergence of new ideas that can inform us on how to move forward for transformation. Traditional power structures (such as teacher as expert and student as empty vessels) act to hide human vulnerabilities that generate the illusion that knowledge and superior leadership dispositions lie within an individual or group that are often attached to identities. Once a teacher provides multiple opportunities for full participation in which authentic interactions occur, people are

> Channeling energy with equity in mind is often removing ourselves from the center of action. This disrupts the power structure by allowing all participants to construct knowledge and meaning.

more likely to see examples of the vulnerability of those with pedagogical authority so that a contrary conviction can begin to grow with them.[3] Removing oneself from the center of action can feel uncomfortable at first. In my experience, teachers always want to fix things and be in control of the learning process. This is because we have been socialized to believe that part of our role as a teacher is to fill gaps and impart knowledge where knowledge does not exist. It is also because teachers are passionate about their subject and often get captivated by it.

Our value for equity needs to drive all action. Mindful action becomes about how we channel our energy in ways that enable us to integrate new ideas, which can only come about through the process of inquiry, observation without judgment, and deliberation. This is more important than leading the change itself. The willingness to reposition ourselves outside the center of all things redistributes power and breaks down notions of ethnocentrism in ways that ensures that the vision and driver of action lies within the people themselves.

Reflection Questions

1. What is the meaning of a retreat? Have you ever experienced a period of inaction that led to clarity of purpose and direction?

2. How does one suspend judgment when one is in the position to observe the practice of others?

3. What does it mean that language and culture are interdependent?

4. Who are in positions of power in your school and school district? How might it look if these positions were redistributed differently to move equity ahead?

5. Are there members of the school or community whose talents are not being recognized or leveraged? How do you know? What would it take to bring the individuals or individual into full participation?

6. How might we design professional development differently so that we can channel our energy in ways that enable us to integrate these new ideas for equity?

Notes

1. Freire, P. (1970). *Pedagogy of the Oppressed. 30th Anniversary Edition* (2003). New York: Continuum, p. 142.
2. Bonilla, R. (1964). *Rationale for a Culturally Based Program of Action for Against Poverty among New York Puerto Ricans.* Avaliable online at: http://files.eric.ed.gov/fulltext/ED011543.pdf
3. Freire, P. (1970). *Pedagogy of the Oppressed. 30th Anniversary Edition* (2003). New York: Continuum, p. 64.

Conclusion

North American Education

> *God bless America, land that I love,*
> *stand beside her, and guide her . . .*

Long before teaching was an option,
when very little, my mother said,
Cuidate, de los buenos quedan poco.

Words that carry stunning assumptions:
there are many bad and a few good ones;
I was a good one; that to remain one,

to simply remain, I would need to take care
of myself.

      Who dreams a three-legged Rin-Tin-Tin
fenced in an abandoned school yard, starving,
dirt orange rust spreading on a frozen chain & lock?
Cuidate, de los buenos quedan poco.
                         Perhaps
I could have questioned my mother: I was good.

Hermano, hermana why not believe we are good?
We are few and need to take care of ourselves;
not let our flag end in shreds on the ground.

Walk by an open school to see children at play;
still see star & stripes flapping in a strong breeze;
My mother meant well, yet missed: see all the good.

Andrés Castro
11/28/2016

More than a decade has passed since I discovered Paulo Freire and his seminal work, *Pedagogy of the Oppressed*.[1] Today, in an interview with Amy Goodman and Nermeen Shaikh on *Democracy Now*, Dr. Cornel West, Professor Emeritus at Princeton University called this "one of the most frightening moments in the history of this very fragile empire and very fragile Republic." In this interview, West explained that people voted for Trump because he "presented himself as caring for their situation; so that economic insecurity, that economic neglect is very real, and it was disproportionally white brothers and sisters, but they are suffering." "It was a cry out from their heart," he said, "and then Trump used that kind of anguish to scapegoat Mexicans, Muslims and others rather than confront the most powerful." He continued on to say that, "there has to be some integrity and moral consistency. Those on the outside of the system, those who are free, are going to tell the truth, we are going to be honest, we are going to have a certain kind of moral and spiritual and intellectual integrity and no matter how marginal that makes us, we are not in any way going to become well adjusted to this injustice."

I ask myself: What now of the magic of Freire's work—that life force that emanates from a book giving a language and critical consciousness to so many? What now of that magic? Freire's pedagogy for conscientization could and arguably should still be applied to how we support and develop teachers in this country, although sadly, the majority of research related to how a teacher develops an identity continues to point to this notion of adaptation to the teaching environment rather than liberation from it.[2] We have for such a long time been operating in an industrial, marketplace, neoliberal mentality in which we can see how in-service teacher practices, in particular, reflect the desire amongst districts to simply reproduce the system, emphasizing current policy.[3] It is not surprising then that critical pedagogy remains an interesting "project" relegated to the urban classroom while educators across the country witness conformity to establishment and neoliberal politics that give rise to neo-fascist ideology.

Krishnamurti wisely said, "My consciousness is the world and the consciousness of the world is me. When there is change in this consciousness it affects the whole consciousness of the world."[4]

When I first internalized Freire's message, my consciousness expanded. Through Freire, I understood the toxic dynamic of the oppressed and the oppressor. His expert analysis of the psyche, language and the dynamics of relationships within the socio-political context is liberating. Yet, years later, I realize the oppressed–oppressor dynamic is still fragmentation and preserves the segregated mind. This duality no longer serves us because as even Freire pointed out, in the duality of roles, the oppressed will often becomes the oppressor, as we see in the Israeli–Palestinian dilemma. How do we let go of the "oppressed–oppressor" dynamic from our consciousness?

Gandhi writes:

Ahimsa (non-violence toward all living things) is the basis of the search for truth. I am realizing every day that the search is vain unless it is founded on ahimsa, as the basis. It is quite proper to resist and attack a system, but to resist and attack its author is tantamount to resisting and attacking oneself. For we are all tarred with the same brush, and are children of one and the same Creator, and as such the divine powers within us are infinite.[5]

When the news of the death of two black men killed by law enforcement hit, one in Tulsa and one in North Carolina, it was business as usual. During a long staff meeting a colleague texts me because equity always feels so abstract, so far away. Can't we do more? I have observed how we are part of a big monster system, marginalized by our own complacency within the same education discourse, and I wonder if our Spirit for action will ever rise above it.

On the day of Trump's election followed by talks of his appointing Stephen Bannon, it became, "this is *not* business as usual."

For two decades, I have been in and out of schools and have worked with nonprofit and private educational organizations. I have observed the same scene playing over and over again. I have become expert at smiling and holding the hands of teachers and leaders while having the same "groundhog" conversations—what can we do? What can we do to solve our equity problem? Sometimes, I'm not very good at "business as usual" and I stay home transfixed. I am transfixed and sullen and then they ask, what has happened to you now? Nothing I reply, I'm just sick or I'm tired. Talking about our suffering and doing the same thing over and over again is not only the definition of insanity but it is the death of my Spirit.

My 13-year-old daughter is a fiction writer and she wrote her first novel last summer. Every day I am in awe of the new generation of children. I tell her I am writing the conclusion for my book and I don't want to summarize my chapters like good, "nonfiction" books do. She smiles at me like I am the child and tells me to just skip the conclusion altogether. My daughter is free. She is not part of the system yet and from the outside, you can speak truthfully and not worry about the implications. Good teachers are free spirits, like the children they teach. They are the artisans of a good life, a beautiful life.

As I write, I am acutely aware that Latino educators often do not get the platform to speak or write for a broad audience in spite of the increasing number of Latino students in our schools across the country. We have actors and writers like Lin-Manuel Miranda of the famous Broadway musical *Hamilton*, who by default became the spokesperson for the Puerto Rican people when Americans got wind of the economic crisis devastating the island of my ancestors. I think about my daughter's wise words about foregoing a proper conclusion and think about the practice of Authentic Presence, Freedom and Emergence. I decide to reach out to a kindred spirit, Dr. Roque Diaz Tizol, who you may remember is the man I met serendipitously in Puerto Rico, the founder and president of COSEY, dedicated to improving the lives of his people through education. I remember standing with Roque outside his office atop a high mountain overlooking Yabucoa, his humble birth town. I remember how he invited me into his home where he and his wife prepared a traditional Puerto Rican meal. On that day, I thought, Roque is the spirit of my grandmother who is welcoming me home.

In the practice of Freedom, I would like to conclude this work with a statement Roque prepared for me when he heard I was nearing the end of my book. I hope that in doing so, I duly express the power of listening to our inner wisdom and honoring the dictates of Spirit Consciousness. In the end, I have found that we are here to listen deeply to each other and honor the unique voice of every human being that crosses our path with reverence and purpose. Therein lies the essence of education—to create those open spaces for us to listen, to honor, to seek truth with courage and faith and to realize that each of us is an integral part of one intelligent whole. This is Conscientious Engagement.

***

Education is the process of tempering the soul for a good and productive life. On this, our great teacher Don Ángel Quintero Alfaro (former Secretary of Education of Puerto Rico and distinguished educator) said, "schools are the workshop where the soul of the people is carved." In both these expressions, educating appeals to the soul of the human being and the soul is directly related to the spirit, that which sustains life. It is what makes the human being strong and makes him aware of what life is and the value of life itself, the common denominator of every organism. Therefore, when spiritual consciousness prevails in the human being, they become respectful of others and live with a great commitment to work for the common good and a genuine appreciation for all manifestations of life. This way of being is projected through self-confidence, acceptance, sense of self-worth, responsibility for one's own existence and social commitment. These attributes begin in family life, but through the process of education, they are encouraged and brought together in such a way that it contributes to the formation of an integrated human being with spiritual consciousness along with other disciplines.

Who is responsible for awakening this spiritual consciousness in the human being? It corresponds, for the most part, as we pointed out, to education. This should be the ultimate and main goal of all education. But how is it achieved? It is up to schools to awaken and cultivate spiritual awareness through socialization and academic processes. These two must be intertwined through processes of the highest quality.

They have to be inclusive based on equity rather than equality. This implies "giving each one what he needs" so that he reaches his spiritual consciousness, which I believe to mean respecting and accepting oneself, respecting others, striving for continuous improvement, as well as making a decisive contribution to the common good. From this point of view, if you ask me: What should schools be like? What type of environment must prevail so that a human being can achieve a sense of purpose and focus on the dream to achieve a better world? I would say that for schools to be effective, they must be holistic and appeal equally to the different dimensions of the human being. This means understanding a child's development is both academics and socialization together. Teaching strategies must be of high quality, inclusive and live within respectful work environments where all humans model a deep spiritual consciousness as well as evaluate the processes at work using equitable measures.

These schools are now more necessary than ever for the children of Puerto Rican immigrant families who are banished from their soil without understanding the reasons and then find it difficult to take root in another soil. They arrive to schools whose environments are not relevant, and they become a number and are asked to work with the same books and answer the same exams. Oh, and most reject them! Far from securing their roots in a new soil, they remain like norias seeking a reason to exist, never assuming responsibility, having no confidence in themselves and passing through life "without knowing what happened."

These children, to rescue them and insert them into the true processes of life, require schools with a high focus on developing and fostering spiritual awareness. For this, as this author says, we need to consider and develop an emerging spiritual consciousness amongst teachers first; to recognize that the struggle for an egalitarian education is part of our human evolution, an evolution that has the power to free us from false ideologies and hegemonies that divide us and invade the consciousness of teachers in particular by political forces and the protection of a larger market; and that this emerging spiritual consciousness has the strength and energy to push teachers—along with various movements in society—towards a broader understanding of education. This holistic education approach is the means by which we can create a new system that focuses more on collective well-being rather than on economic divisions and races. It is that education that will make us free. The staff who teaches this must possess these attributes themselves and the school environment must provide for them the right environment, teaching materials and strategies that will promote the achievement of this aspiration. To achieve an education whose optimal aim is to contribute to the formation of human beings with a great spiritual consciousness is valuable indeed.

***

Notes

1. Interestingly, Freire is foundational in all education curricula in Latin America and beyond. US education's canon, however, remains predominately Western with McLaren, Giroux and Darder introducing Freire through their critical theory and critical pedagogy work.
2. Blankenship, R.J. (2013). Teacher as object to teacher as subject: A critical perspective of teacher training in the 21st century. *International Journal of University Teaching and Faculty Development*, Vol. 4, No. 1, pp. 27–43.
3. Ibid.
4. Krishnamurti, J. (1973). *The Awakening of Intelligence*. New York: Harper One, An Imprint of Harper Collins Publishers.
5. Gandhi, M.K. (1983). *Mohandas K. Gandhi Autobiography: The Story of My Experiments with Truth*. New York: Dover Publications, p. 242.

Taylor & Francis eBooks

Helping you to choose the right eBooks for your Library

Add Routledge titles to your library's digital collection today. Taylor and Francis ebooks contains over 50,000 titles in the Humanities, Social Sciences, Behavioural Sciences, Built Environment and Law.

Choose from a range of subject packages or create your own!

Benefits for you

» Free MARC records
» COUNTER-compliant usage statistics
» Flexible purchase and pricing options
» All titles DRM-free.

Benefits for your user

» Off-site, anytime access via Athens or referring URL
» Print or copy pages or chapters
» Full content search
» Bookmark, highlight and annotate text
» Access to thousands of pages of quality research at the click of a button.

REQUEST YOUR **FREE** INSTITUTIONAL TRIAL TODAY

Free Trials Available
We offer free trials to qualifying academic, corporate and government customers.

eCollections – Choose from over 30 subject eCollections, including:

Archaeology	Language Learning
Architecture	Law
Asian Studies	Literature
Business & Management	Media & Communication
Classical Studies	Middle East Studies
Construction	Music
Creative & Media Arts	Philosophy
Criminology & Criminal Justice	Planning
Economics	Politics
Education	Psychology & Mental Health
Energy	Religion
Engineering	Security
English Language & Linguistics	Social Work
Environment & Sustainability	Sociology
Geography	Sport
Health Studies	Theatre & Performance
History	Tourism, Hospitality & Events

For more information, pricing enquiries or to order a free trial, please contact your local sales team:
www.tandfebooks.com/page/sales

Routledge
Taylor & Francis Group

The home of
Routledge books

www.tandfebooks.com